D1663114

Citlali Ayala Martínez | Ulrich Müller [eds.]

Towards Horizontal Cooperation and Multi-Partner Collaboration

Knowledge Sharing and Development Cooperation in
Latin America and the Caribbean

Deutsche Gesellschaft für Internationale
Zusammenarbeit (GIZ) GmbH
Asia/ Pacific and Latin America/
Carribbean Department
P.O. Box 5180
65726 Eschborn, Germany
www.giz.de

Instituto de Investigaciones
Dr. José María Luis Mora
Plaza Valentín Gómez Farías 12
Col. San Juan Mixcoac
Delegación Benito Juárez
03730 Ciudad de México
México
www.mora.edu.mx

The opinions and analyses expressed in this book do not necessarily reflect the opinion of the editors nor the views and official policies of GIZ and Instituto Mora.

© Coverpicture: San Miguel de Allende, Mexico, Ulrich Müller, August 2014.

Die Deutsche Nationalbibliothek lists this publication in the
Deutsche Nationalbibliografie; detailed bibliographic data
is available in the Internet at http://dnb.d-nb.de

ISBN   978-3-8487-4713-9 (Nomos Print)
          978-3-8452-8942-7 (Nomos ePDF)

British Library Cataloguing-in-Publication Data
A catalogue record for this book is available from the British Library.

ISBN   978-3-8487-4713-9 (Nomos Print)
          978-3-8452-8942-7 (Nomos ePDF)

Library of Congress Cataloging-in-Publication Data
Ayala Martínez, Citlali / Müller, Ulrich
Towards Horizontal Cooperation and Multi-Partner Collaboration
Knowledge Sharing and Development Cooperation in Latin America and the Caribbean
Citlali Ayala Martínez / Ulrich Müller (eds.)
180 p.
Includes bibliographic references.

ISBN   978-3-8487-4713-9 (Nomos Print)
          978-3-8452-8942-7 (Nomos ePDF)
ISBN   978-607-9475-73-4 (Instituto de Investigaciones Dr. José María Luis Mora)

1st Edition 2017
© Nomos Verlagsgesellschaft, Baden-Baden, Germany 2017. Printed and bound in Germany.

Preface

Recent emphasis placed on Knowledge Sharing in international development cooperation may make the practice seem like one more new trend, like so many others that that have come and gone over the past decades; a new label placed on a nonetheless almost unchanged practice. This publication provides some answers as to why Knowledge Sharing should be considered more than a passing fad: Knowledge Sharing in development cooperation poses constant challenges but has the potential to make a difference in the form of substantial change and an alternative to the promises of easy ways and shortcuts generally made by other new trends.

A first reason why Knowledge Sharing is different lies in the fact that it represents a genuine effort to bring South-South and North-South cooperation together. For decades, both cooperation forms coexisted without major points of contact, often doing similar types of work but with very different reference systems and languages and remarkable sets of mutual prejudices. It is the notion of sharing, of taking the other seriously as a bearer of knowledge and experience, a genuine interest in one's partner that allows bridging this divide between those who should be natural partners. Such horizontal partnership corresponds with the increased self-esteem of emerging countries and with the requirements of global challenges, which face all countries to varying degrees. This is the idea of universality adopted in the 2030 Agenda for Sustainable Development: all countries are partners on equal terms, all are learners and all have something to provide.

A second factor making Knowledge Sharing an interesting topic for international development cooperation is its close relationship to insights on the nature of learning processes made during the past decades. Learning requires more than just knowledge on the characteristics of a determined subject area. It also demands the ability to move from understanding to doing, something that is often easier learned with the hands than with the head. At the same time, learning is also bound to underlying worldviews, value systems and attitudes, which rather come from the heart and include emotional dimensions and the use of all senses. Apart from subject area competence, this requires personal, social and methodological competences, which go hand in hand and nurture one another. Although the word "knowledge" forms part of its name, Knowledge Sharing comprises all these dimensions of learning. Finally, it also takes into account that learning is not only something done by persons, but also within organisations and societies.

The third reason Knowledge Sharing merits special attention lies in the wide range of its use. It ranges from daily routines, such as agricultural cultivation practices, to complex issues in the organisation of countries and societies, such as the elaboration of a new constitution. It also allows relating both. In a world, where climate changes not only in a sense of natural science and ecology, but also in social and political relations, such ways of connecting and working together are more necessary than ever. Although spheres of sovereignty and specialisation continue to be necessary for organizing the complex tasks faced by human communities, isolation is not an option. Instead, there is a need to communicate and exchange, maintaining respect for the specific characteristics of communities while also promoting the openness to adapt new ideas and practices.

From a practitioner's point of view, Knowledge Sharing always has been a part of successful cooperation projects, but that also has always been hard to achieve. This is why Knowledge Sharing may not appear new to someone with strong field experience in international development cooperation, but on the other hand will always be unfamiliar when entering a different context and tackling an unknown challenge. This publication strives to deepen views on these experiences by combining both practitioners' and scientists' points of view. It is the fruit of a well-established South-North partnership between the Mexican think tank Instituto Mora and the German implementation organisation of sustainable development, GIZ. As such, it is not only a book about Knowledge Sharing, but also a product of Knowledge Sharing between editors and authors from different backgrounds and continents. It is also one of a series of books on new cooperation forms in international development cooperation that started in 2012 with an edition on triangular cooperation, followed in 2014 with a volume on global funds and networks.

Many thanks to the authors and editors for making this in depth reading on Knowledge Sharing possible and best wishes to all readers, in the hopes that you will find within these pages an inspiring read that relates to what you are doing in practice.

Eschborn, November 2017

Annette Bähring, Director of the Methodological Approaches Division, Deutsche Gesellschaft für Internationale Zusammenarbeit (GIZ) GmbH

Martina Vahlhaus, Director of the Central America and Caribbean Division, Deutsche Gesellschaft für Internationale Zusammenarbeit (GIZ) GmbH

Contents

List of Abbreviations

ACODE	Advocates Coalition for Development and Environment
ACP	African, Caribbean and Pacific Group of States
AFI	Alliance for Financial Inclusion
AIAMP	Asociación Ibero Americana de Ministerios Públicos Ibero-American Association of Public Prosecutors
AIZ	Akademie für Internationale Zusammenarbeit Academy for International Cooperation
AMEXCID	Agencia Mexicana de Cooperación Internacional para el Desarrollo Mexican Agency for International Development Cooperation
BMZ	Bundesministerium für wirtschaftliche Zusammenarbeit und Entwicklung German Federal Ministry for Economic Cooperation and Development
CA	Constituent Assembly
CAN	Andean Community of Nations
CAR	Corporación Autónoma Regional de Cundinamarca Autonomous Regional Corporation of Bogotá and Cundinamarca, Colombia
CARICOM	Caribbean Community
CARIFORUM	Caribbean Forum
CCAFS	Program for Research on Climate Change, Agriculture and Food Security
CIAT	Centro Internacional de Agricultura Tropical International Centre for Tropical Agriculture, Colombia
CDB	Carribean Development Bank
CEOSC	Confederación Ecuatoriana de Organizaciones de la Sociedad Civil Ecuadorian Confederation of Civil Society Organisations
CEHI	Caribbean Environmental Health Institute
CEP	Comparative Evidence Paper
CGIAR	Consultative Group for International Agricultural Research
CONABIO	Comisión Nacional para el Conocimiento y Uso de la Biodiversidad National Commission for Biodiversity Study and Use, Mexico
CONAMAQ	Consejo Nacional de Ayllus y Markas del Qullasuyu Council of Ayllus and Marqas of Collasuyu, Bolivia
COP10	10th Conference of the Parties
COSUDE	Cooperación Suiza de Desarrollo Swiss Agency for Development and Cooperation
CRIP	Caribbean Regional Indicative Programme
CSO	Civil Society Organisation

9

CSUTCB	Confederación Sindical Única de Trabajadores Campesinos de Bolivia
	Single Confederation of Unions of Rural Workers of Bolivia
CXC	Caribbean Examinations Council
DFID	Department for International Development, UK
ECLAC	Economic Commission for Latin America and Caribbean
EDF	European Development Fund
EIP	Extractive Industries Program
EITI	Extractive Industries Transparency Initiative
ELLA	Evidence and Lessons from Latin America
EPRS	European Parliamentary Research Service
EU	European Union
FARO	Fundación para el Avance de las Reformas y las Oportunidades
	Foundation for the Advance of Reforms and Opportunities, Ecuador
FIDA	Fondo Internacional de Desarrollo Agrícola
	International Fund for Agricultural Development
FIO	Federación Iberoamericana del Ombudsman
	Ibero-American Federation of Ombudsman
FNMC-BS	Federación National de Mujeres Campesinas "Bartolina Sisa"
	National Federation of Rural Women, Bolivia
GDP	Gross Domestic Product
GIZ	Deutsche Gesellschaft für Internationale Zusammenarbeit GmbH
	German Agency for International Cooperation
GNI	Gross National Income
GPKS	Global Partnership on Country-led Knowledge Sharing
GPF	Global Policy Forum
GPFI	Global Partnership for Financial Inclusion
IADB	Inter-American Development Bank
IATI	International Aid Transparency Initiative
ICT4Ag	Information and Communications Technology for Agriculture
IDEAM	Instituto de Hidrología, Meteorología y Estudios Ambientales
	Institute of Meteorology, Hydrology and Environmental Studies, Colombia
IDRC	International Development Research Centre
IDS	Institute of Development Studies, UK
IMF	International Monetary Fund
ILAIPP	Iniciativa Latinoamericana de Investigación para las Políticas Públicas
	Latin American Network for Public Policy Research

INTN	Instituto Nacional de Tecnología, Normalización y Metrología National Institute of Technology, Normalisation and Metrology, Paraguay
IPCC	Intergovernmental Panel on Climate Change
IsDB	Islamic Development Bank
IWCAM	Integrating Watershed and Coastal Area Management
JICA	Japanese International Cooperation Agency
KDI	Korean Development Institute
KM	Knowledge Management
LAC	Latin America and Caribbean
LCID	Ley de Cooperación Internacional para el Desarrollo Law of International Development Cooperation, Mexico
LEA	Learning Alliance
M&E	Monitoring & Evaluation
MADR	Ministerio de Agricultura y Desarrollo Rural Ministry of Agriculture and Rural Development, Colombia
MAS	Movimiento al Socialismo Movement for Socialism, Bolivia
MDG	Millennium Development Goals
MDRyT	Ministerio de Desarrollo Rural y Tierras Ministry for Rural and Land Development, Bolivia
MU	Management Unit
MTAs	Mesas Técnicas Agroclimáticas Agro-Climate Technical Forums
NGO	Non-government Organisation
OECD	Organisation for Economic Co-operation and Development
OIC	Organisation for Islamic Cooperation
OLACEFS	Organización Latinoamericana y del Caribe de Entidades Fiscalizadoras Superiors Organisation of Latin American and Caribbean Supreme Audit Institutions
PAC	Practical Action Consulting
PAHO	Pan American Health Organisation
PCS	Political Constitution of the State
PDVSA	Petróleos de Venezuela S.A. Venezuela's National Oil Company
PROSUCO	Asociación Promoción de la Sustentabilidad y Conocimientos Compartidos Association for the Promotion of Sustainability and Shared Knowledge
R+D+i	Research, Techological Development and Innovation

11

REDD+	Reducing Emissions from Deforestation and Forest Degradation and the Role of Conservation, Sustainable Management of Forests and Enhancement of Forest Carbon Stocks in Developing Countries
REP	Regional Evidence Paper
RELASER	Red Latinoamericana de Servicios de Extensión Rural Latin American Network of Rural Extension Services
RENCID	Registro Nacional de Cooperación Internacional para el Desarrollo National Registry of International Development Cooperation, Mexico
RLIE	Red Latinoamericana sobre las Industrias Extracticas Latin American Network for Extractives Industries
SAB-UNGA	Scientific Advisory Board of the United Nations General Assembly
SEGIB	Secretaria General Iberoamericana Ibero-American Program
SDG	Sustainable Development Goals
SICA	Sistema de la Integración Centroamericana Central American Integration System
SIM	Sistema Interamericano de Metrologiá Inter-american Metrology System
TNC	The Nature Conservancy
UKCIF	UK Caribbean Infrastructure Partnership Fund
UMATA	Unidades Municipales de Asistencia Técnica Agropecuaria Municipal Technical Assistance Units, Colombia
UN	United Nations
UNDP	United Nations Development Programme
UNEP	United Nations Environment Programme
UNESCO	United Nations Educational, Scientific and Cultural Organisation
CIRAN	Centre for Intenational Research and Advisory Networks
UNODC	United Nations Office on Drugs and Crime
UNOPS	United Nations Office for Project Services
USAID	United States Agency for International Development
VDRA	Viceministerio de Desarrollo Rural y Agropecuario Vice Ministry of Rural and Agricultural Development, Bolivia

Introduction

Citlali Ayala Martínez and Ulrich Müller

Knowledge Sharing has become a buzzword in international development cooperation. It draws attention to two aspects that have always been present in both South-South and North-South cooperation experiences, but which have also proved challenging in most cases.

The first aspect is knowledge. Knowledge is important because mere financing and infrastructure are not sufficient to produce the desired developmental changes. However, where does this knowledge come from? The idea that knowledge has to be transferred from the global centres to the global periphery disregards the many inventions that come from the periphery, and the richness and value of ancestral knowledge that humanity cannot dismiss. Does knowledge only consist of what can be registered systematically in encyclopedic collections of words, or could it also be embedded in hands and bodies, beliefs and worldviews? Is knowledge unique and compounded in one scientific truth, or is it necessarily fragmented and always contextual? Is knowledge something that can be possessed and taken home in textbooks or memory sticks, or is it something that has to be learned anew every day, questioned, reaffirmed, rearranged, deepened, enlarged and focused again?

The second aspect is sharing. One of the most important lessons learned in international development cooperation is that development cannot be brought from outside. Development is a task to be mastered by persons, organisations and societies for themselves. In other words: persons, organisations and societies have to take ownership of their own development[1]. This being the case, a mere logic of one-sided transfer cannot reach very far. For ownership to be possible, there needs to be a two-sided flow of ideas and a mutual respect between partners, a relationship of sharing rather than transfer. But the word sharing may even reach further. Sharing means to give something without interest, handing over without fearing a loss of property rights and without attempting to control what the other will do with

---

1   Regarding the importance of ownership in international development cooperation, see for instance Leutner/Müller 2010.

what is shared. Hence, the idea of a sharing economy is subject to much criticism in the context of dominant capitalist practices.

Within this broad framework – too broad to be explored in a single collection of texts - this book aims to demonstrate how recent Knowledge Sharing initiatives in Latin America and the Caribbean have contributed to the transformation of development cooperation into multi-actor partnerships for tackling global challenges. This discussion takes place within the framework of the new 2030 Agenda for Sustainable Development. It coincides with a fundamental change in international and development cooperation characterized by an increasing need for joint action between traditional donors and recipients to address global challenges, and to protect and promote global public goods. This requires a shift from the old paradigm of aid towards more equity-based, horizontal, demand-driven approaches and cooperation forms.

In parallel with traditional donors' partial withdrawal from engagement in emerging countries, the latter are now taking on more international responsibility. South-South Cooperation and Triangular Cooperation, which involves partners from both North and South, are two more recent approaches that have opened space for new experiences and practices. This context raises another key issue: at the heart of Agenda 2030 is the notion that economic and social development will only be possible through the joint efforts of public institutions, Non-government Organisations (NGOs), academia and the private sector under effective governance.

Knowledge Sharing takes place among different actors within countries and in bilateral and multilateral exercises. It helps to connect different communities – for example, the academia with development practitioners/epistemic communities, or practitioners with decision makers. This process must be linked in the long term to the implementation of public policies. The demand for Knowledge Sharing is not only a demand to connect with new partners or to collect and analyse information, but also to benefit from each other's practical experiences of the "how-to" of development and policy reform in mutual learning processes, and to co-create innovative solutions. A central claim of this book is that those features nurture and transform Knowledge Sharing into a form of cooperation that is constantly changing, expanding (both conceptually and practically), and which can be better understood through detailed case studies from different regions in the world, our contribution coming from Latin America and the Caribbean. The aim is to analyse the mind-set of Knowledge Sharing from theory to practice.

The current debate on knowledge and Knowledge Sharing is very diverse. It ranges from questions regarding the production of knowledge in social theory and philosophy of science[2] to technological issues of digital data processing and storage. There is also a close link to topics of data security, protection of privacy and intellectual property rights, as well as commons-based peer production of knowledge[3]. In one way or another, all these dimensions also relate to the issues of development and development cooperation that are the focus of this book. Nevertheless, it is simply not possible in a single volume to shed light on all these dimensions and linkages. Any attempt to compile such content must inevitably be somewhat arbitrary and incomplete. The same holds true regarding the present selection of chapters.

This book comprises two types of contributions. The first conceptualizes Knowledge Sharing and its links to International Development Cooperation. The second explores case studies from Latin America and the Caribbean, showing the power of Knowledge Sharing to forge ties between South-South and North-South partners, the new roles of experts in Knowledge Sharing, the point of view of the indigenous population and regional experiences in the Caribbean and Central America.

The book itself can be considered a Knowledge Sharing exercise, since it unites authors with a range of academic or practice oriented backgrounds who also represent a range of different interpretations of the concepts of knowledge and Knowledge Sharing. Thus, the way Knowledge Sharing is addressed corresponds with the specific characteristics of the topic, while no claim is made of offering absolute truths on the subject of Knowledge Sharing. Instead, we have limited ourselves to collecting different opinions that enter a kind of dialogue, allowing readers to form their own opinions. The variety of perspectives provides richness, and learning will likely be the result of this diversity, rather than proven truths.

Apart from already published sources, the text is also enriched by personal experience, tacit knowledge and insights into institutional debates that are generally not open to the public. The authors bring their personal experience of Knowledge Sharing in the intersection between the academic and practical spheres, from development cooperation to diplomacy. Each author has his or her own particular tone and point of view. Although this may demand more of the reader, these differences have been preserved by the editors. As such, the following chapters may be perceived as the starting point of a mosaic that can grow through further research.

---

2   See for instance Kuhn 1962; Foucault 1970; Habermas 1995.
3   On that topic, see for instance Seibold 2014.

Finally, the book is also the result of living experience of successful South-North collaboration between the editors themselves, which has already yielded fruit. It is a collaboration based on the conviction that learning has to be multidirectional and that empowerment to share and learn must start in oneself if the message of knowledge is to be authentic and credible.

Chapter one by Citlali Ayala explains how a new narrative enlightens the evolution of knowledge transfer to Knowledge Sharing and experience exchange, including mutual learning and decision-making processes, from North-South to South-South and among development partners, from bilateral relations to multipolar networks, including private and public partnerships. This shows that knowledge is equally valuable whether its origin is in the North or the South. Every country has something to offer and needs something from someone else. Horizontal and inclusive associations in the South are able to diversify and produce knowledge in ways that go beyond common patterns seen in industrialized countries, showcasing southern sources for development solutions.

In the second chapter, Ulrich Müller shows that there are good reasons why Knowledge Sharing has been the subject of increased interest in the area of international development cooperation, and examines why it is nevertheless applied less than could be expected. He explores possible roles in four fields of competences that make up the spirit – or the art – of Knowledge Sharing, finally placing Knowledge Sharing in the context of current trends in international development cooperation.

In third place, Iris Barth, Ulrich Müller and Anna Fiedler take a deeper look at the added value of Knowledge Sharing and how it can be measured. In order to achieve this purpose, they introduce two concepts of learning. The first emphasizes that learning is not only a matter of knowledge, but also of ability and attitude. The second refers to the different implications of learning at the level of persons, organisations and societies. Based on these concepts they form a matrix of different types of added value in Knowledge Sharing.

The following chapter depicts the experiences of Grupo FARO (Fundación para el Avance de las Reformas y las Oportunidades), the Ecuadorian research partner of the Evidence and Lessons from Latin America program (ELLA). Here, Marcela Morales and Melani Peláez seek to contribute a Latin American and practical perspective on Knowledge Sharing among experts' networks in a cross-continental perspective with Africa. They analyse how this interesting experience contributes to closing the literature gap on practical experiences from Ecuador and Latin America around this topic, bearing some scholarly points of view on Knowledge Sharing in advocacy networks and epistemic communities.

Following the presentation of successful experiences, Horacio Rodríguez introduces the reader to the field of innovation in the rural sector in general and agricultural activities in particular. He explores how the concept of agricultural extension spread to Latin America and the Caribbean and how the flow of information, technology and knowledge goes from research centers and academic institutions toward landholders and back. An interesting perspective here is the work with indigenous populations, where knowledge exchange takes on a particular tone, which is influenced by a number of factors, ranging from language barriers to worldview, belief system and local culture, including self-management processes and decision-making within a particular community.

Chapter six, written by Iván Égido, continues the analysis of experiences with indigenous communities, their relationships with others and the results derived from these. He argues that the learning, exchange and negotiation of knowledge are practices that exist across human cultures, to which indigenous cultures are no exception. His focus describes strategies they have employed in the process of exchanging and sharing their knowledge and experiences in the political field, specifically while working toward obtaining recognition of their collective rights during the process of drafting the Bolivian constitution of 2009.

Moving towards formal formats for managing the exchange of experiences, Iván Sierra takes us to the Caribbean, exploring the current situation affecting Caribbean countries as a region that is characterized by the complex convergence of harsh economic realities, political factors, and social trends that present profound challenges to national governments. He argues that there is a need for innovative instruments of international development cooperation in order to activate the strategic interventions that are required to jumpstart change. After discussing recent experiences of international development cooperation intervention in the area, he analyses lessons learned and possible challenges ahead in the evolving practice of international development cooperation in the Caribbean.

Citlali Ayala Martínez and Ulrich Müller

Acknowledgements

We would like to thank all authors for their contributions to this book, as well as all colleagues at Instituto Mora and the German Agency for International Cooperation (GIZ) who supported this work, especially Penelope McKimm and Judith Rehr for their assistance in language revision and text editing.

Bibliography

Foucault, Michel (1970): The Order of Things: An Archaeology of the Human Sciences, Pantheon, New York City.

Habermas, Jürgen (1981): Theorie des kommunikativen Handelns, Suhrkamp, Frankfurt am Main.

Kuhn, Thomas Samuel (1962): The Structure of Scientific Revolutions, University of Chicago Press, Chicago.

Leutner, Jana/Müller, Ulrich (2010): Ownership in Practice, in: Frenken, Sarah/Müller, Ulrich (eds.): Ownership and Political Steering in Developing Countries. Proceedings of international conferences in London and Berlin, Nomos, Baden-Baden, p. 47-59.

Seibold, Balthas (2014): Learning by Sharing. How global communities cultivate skills and capacity through peer-production of knowledge, Deutsche Gesellschaft für Internationale Zusammenarbeit, Bonn.

Evolution of Knowledge Sharing: Increasing the Potential of Development Actors in a Challenging Environment

Citlali Ayala Martínez

Introduction

The definition of Knowledge Sharing is broad and constantly evolving, as will be shown further on. Some key words that briefly outline the concept and its current practices include Knowledge Management, knowledge and experiences exchange, systematic accumulation of knowledge, research, knowledge and information organization, access to information, knowledge transfer and dissemination, bilateral exchange, and so on. Knowledge Sharing has come to be known as a bilateral and multilateral practice amongst public and private development actors, prevalent in epistemic communities, an increasingly plural group of actors and professionals in the fields of development (including science and technology), business and social relations.

Commonly used for many decades either as knowledge transfer or Knowledge Management, Knowledge Sharing has become an acknowledged practice between North and South, involving processes of mutual learning aimed at horizontal dialogues. It will be shown that, in contrast with knowledge transfer, Knowledge Sharing stands for horizontal relationships, diminishing hierarchical structures and proposing mutual learning among practitioners and development actors.

This chapter explores how a new narrative has emerged that includes the evolution from knowledge transfer to Knowledge Sharing and experience exchange, as well as mutual learning processes, from North-South to South-South and among development partners, from bilateral relations to multipolar networks, including private and public partnerships. Latin America and the Caribbean are current partners in these kinds of processes, both in theoretical debate and in practice, therefore, it is necessary to analyse their experiences as sources of new input for the current debate.

The text consists of three parts: the first provides a conceptual exploration of Knowledge Sharing, by way of experiences with technical cooperation in recent history; the second analyses the connection between

Knowledge Sharing policy and practice in Southern countries. Finally, the third explains some advantages and constraints of Knowledge Sharing in the practice of South-South cooperation.

Conceptual analysis of Knowledge Sharing and its links with development and technical cooperation

In presenting the background ideas on Knowledge Sharing, a range of different voices should be heard, from international organisations to the academia and civil society.

The action of Knowledge Sharing is possible under organized or non-organized conditions, either bilaterally or between multiple actors. It is also done by organisations subject to international law, civil associations, CSOs (Civil Society Organisations), academic and scientific institutions, governments, and the private sector. Knowledge is one of the intrinsic values of networks, with the various means of communication as its basic vehicle. Nowadays, knowledge transfer and experience exchange use digital platforms and rely mostly in information technologies. Knowledge Sharing also relies heavily on practitioner-run workshops and academic seminars to spread its methodologies, specific knowledge and techniques, usually related to social and economic development, as well as social practices for political processes. More importantly, it has enhanced the links between public policies and the implementation of development solutions.

Over time, it has been common for different actors and management teams to engender epistemic and research communities, whether regional, local or global. This might lead them toward integration and cooperation. From technical cooperation to capacity development, supported by Knowledge Sharing within South-South and Triangular Cooperation, Knowledge Sharing has evolved on international, regional, national, subnational and local levels, within bilateral, triangular or multipolar frameworks, and is related to information technology, innovation, and science and technology.

Based on findings by Angus Maddison, it can be said that Knowledge Sharing was initially understood and aligned to the idea that

"the effective planning of technical assistance, required a wide view of human resources and the educational national strategy of the beneficiary country, plus an analysis of the efficiency to use its own abilities and training resources, either domestic ones or coming from abroad whether from technical assistance or other resources".[1]

Therefore, planning technical assistance had to start with a stock of domestically-sourced skills in the developing country, as well as determining where gaps existed with respect to the economic structure. Regarding this idea, information, technical knowledge and technical assistance were strongly associated with the education system in the beneficiary country. Complementing this perspective, the decades-long view of assistance that predominated in technical cooperation assumed an absolute vertical perspective.

This technical cooperation was intended and designed to provide a one-way transfer of much needed capacity, in the form of knowledge or technology, from sources that are external to the local context. Although Knowledge Sharing can be related to development cooperation or other fields such as economics, science and technology, this text presupposes an intrinsic link with roots in development cooperation.

Based on the findings of King and McGrath, it can be argued that Knowledge Sharing has always been a major element of the rationale and activities of development cooperation.[2] This has been demonstrated by actions of technical cooperation, bi-directional cooperation, training and technological transfer. However, as these authors point out, the nature, extent and modalities of Knowledge Sharing have undergone substantial changes in the past decade, although significant elements of the changes remain rhetorical at this point. Despite being relatively recent phenomena, the rise of global networks, epistemic communities and inclusive partnerships can support this argument, as well as the increase of creative industries in South-South cooperation.

In the second half of the 1990s, the modalities and specific activities of development cooperation in both multi- and bi-lateral contexts allow us to see how practices of technical cooperation evolved towards certain aspects related to knowledge-based aid. This tendency toward change came mostly from traditional cooperation agencies, but was also due to globalisation and the emergence of the knowledge-based economy.

Kevin King and Simon McGrath argue that, by the mid-1990s, a new management literature was emerging based on the notion of Knowledge Management (KM), concerned with how businesses could manage their

---

1   Maddison 1965: 8.
2   King/McGrath 2004.

knowledge resources, leading to increased competitiveness and profitability. Subsequently, in 1996, World Bank President James Wolfensohn announced the idea of the knowledge bank as a central element of the Strategic Compact[3] designed to restructure the Bank and its work. In this context of strategic planning and institutional organisation, the concept of Knowledge Sharing gradually became a trend supported by development agencies, development banks and the private sector in the developed world.

For instance, as explained by Caroline Wiedenhof and Henk Molenaar, from the early nineties until relatively recently, policy on research for development was characterized by a strong focus on demand orientation and Southern ownership[4], as can be seen in the Dutch case. Therefore, development challenges could be addressed by conducting trans-disciplinary research, given that the interest was in building southern research capacity, including in management and research funding. Thus, the articulation of an authentic Southern research agenda is a prime concern.

Knowledge Sharing was used by bilateral and multilateral agencies in the late nineties, as well as Knowledge Management, considering that certain topics – aid among them – became knowledge-based, in addition to those activities derived from technical and economic cooperation. Subsequently, in the early 2000s donor agencies and development banks began to show preference for Knowledge Sharing, considering that transformations could be achieved by both staff and partners.

In the field of global governance, the G20 has been working on Knowledge Sharing as a way of addressing development issues along with its more established practices. For the G20, Knowledge Sharing as a concept is different from technical assistance or technical cooperation.[5] Whereas technical cooperation can include elements of Knowledge Sharing which, indeed, forms a major part of the technical cooperation programs of some non-traditional development assistance providers, the larger share of technical cooperation is essentially different from Knowledge Sharing.

Ulrich Müller, Lena Lázaro and Citlatli Ayala explored "hybrid actors", independent of traditional development actors, analyzing global funds and networks as potential spaces for supporting processes such as the implementation of global development guidelines, providing financial resources

---

3   World Bank 1997, as cited in King/McGrath 2004.
4   Wiedenhof/Molenaar 2006.
5   G20 2011.

and technical knowledge, and promoting international norms and methodologies.[6] Hence, these global mechanisms can assume the role of facilitators between national and global spheres through the practice of Knowledge Sharing.

Subsequently, Citlali Ayala and Ulrich Müller argue that development cooperation can open many opportunities for development initiatives as well as mutual learning[7], and lead to sharing of both financial resources and knowledge. Moreover, global funds and networks seem to be ideal instruments for this purpose, since funds support development financing and networks foster the exchange of knowledge and experience.

Another essential point is ownership, which has been widely promoted with the implementation of the Paris Declaration and the five principles for aid effectiveness. Thereon, Jana Leutner and Ulrich Müller defined ownership as societies and individuals assuming responsibility for their own development[8]; hence, ownership is not only a favorable condition for implementing policies, but also for potential cooperation among partners.

Over the years, Knowledge Sharing practices have been aimed at development issues in southern countries and, as a result, power and participation have gained importance as objects of research by scholars and policy makers. In recognition of the unequal power relations in research partnerships, and in development cooperation as a whole, an attempt was made to place ownership entirely in southern hands.[9]

An emphasis must be made on degree to which knowledge is embedded into social processes and interactions with stakeholders, due to the potential for researchers, social actors and entrepreneurs of social development to exert an influence over policy-making processes and structures open for democratic participation. For this purpose, it is necessary for donors to understand the context in which knowledge is to be shared, just as stakeholders must understand the process of Knowledge Sharing, its stages and ways to foster ownership. In achieving this ideal, old patterns and paternalistic attitudes would gradually be removed.

Along the same lines, Carlos Parker argues that since the mid-nineties, information technology industries have re-oriented their strategy for generating value based on appropriate Knowledge Management and intellectual

---

6   Lázaro et al. 2014.
7   Ayala/Müller 2014.
8   Leutner/Müller 2010.
9   Wiedenhof/Molenaar 2006.

capital.[10] This is supported by acknowledging their role as a rationale for continuous learning, essential for the sustainability of organisations and the search of new business opportunities. Therefore, Knowledge Management itself would allow organizations to add value to their own processes, products and services.

Taking another ground position, around 2011 the G20 supported the Development Working Group under Pillar 9, which developed the following three-point definition of Knowledge Sharing (2011):

- "sharing of development models and solutions which have proven successful in one or several countries, and might be, in partnership, transferred and adapted in other/s"
- "direct access to valuable and hard-to-codify information on public policies for development constructed on evidence-based approaches, built on the expertise of policy makers and practitioners"
- "a process whereby people, organisations and society, adapt knowledge generated by others to strengthen their own capacity over time as an effective tool for sustainable development and generation of results"[11]

Considering these interpretations as valid and complementary, it is important to analyse the actors and conditions making Knowledge Sharing possible. Terms like knowledge broker have come onto the scene in recent years and it is not certain whether it has been embedded and understood by the full, diverse range of development actors, especially Southern and non-governmental actors. It is possible that some of these actors carry out the tasks of a knowledge broker without naming themselves as such.

That being said, it is necessary to keep in mind global guidelines from multilateral and national organisations, as well as the voices of other global governance groups. The G20 Development Working Group specified the strategy at the Multi-Year Action Plan on Development, which encouraged international organisations to broaden sources of knowledge towards growth and development[12], agreeing to mainstream it to other pillars of development. This has implied focusing institutional efforts towards reinforcing technical cooperation along with more traditional forms, as well as the strategic involvement of technical personnel, twinning arrangements, training and learning opportunities, education and technical equipment. Given

---

10   Parker 2007.
11   World Bank 2015: 19.
12   Ibid.

that this multilateral plan is derived from technical and financial resources in developed and emerging countries, two basic types of technical cooperation were addressed (2011):

> "(1) free-standing technical cooperation (FTC), which is the provision of resources aimed at the transfer of technical and managerial skills or of technology for building up overall national capacity without reference to the implementation of any specific investment projects; and (2) investment-related technical cooperation (IRTC), which denotes the provision of technical services required for the implementation of specific investment projects."[13]

The duty of matching knowledge supply and demand and facilitating the exchange of experiences has taken many forms, such as workshops, seminars, digital platforms, and so on. Once the platform is established, the next tentative steps are generating a decision-making process and the implementation of elements previously chosen from exchanged experiences and knowledge, which, by the way, might have different approaches and means. In any case, it is necessary to ensure leadership, teamwork and some sort of protocol. It is equally important to direct these efforts to leverage public policies.

All this is coherent with the trend towards a knowledge-based economy, on which Carlos Parker points out that knowledge has become the key element for comparative advantage. At the same time, knowledge is simply one more factor of production (beyond land, labor and capital), but one of the current means for boosting development. From the same perspective, Parker revisits the OECD (Organisation for Economic Co-operation and Development) classification of knowledge as follows:

- "Know-what (about the facts and basic information)"
- "Know-why (basis of technological development and advances in products and industrial processes)"
- "Know-how (abilities and capacities within the limits of an organisation; main purpose of networks and elements for sharing)"
- "Know-who (who knows what and how to do what; involves the creation of social networks to allow efficient access to and use of knowledge; the outcome of a social practice which may not always be shared by formal communication channels)"[14]

---

13   Ibid.: 19-20.
14   Parker 2007: 95.

The question of whether Knowledge Sharing is a widely utilized term is in contrast with the ideas proposed below in Dan Paulin and Kaj Suneson's two-point definition:

- "The exchange of knowledge between and among individuals, and within and among teams, organisational units, and organisations. This exchange can be focused or unfocused, but it usually does not have a clear a priori objective."
- "An exchange of knowledge between two individuals: one that communicates knowledge and another that assimilates it. In Knowledge Sharing, the focus is on human capital and the interaction of individuals. Strictly speaking, knowledge can never be shared. Because it exists in a context; the receiver interprets it in the light of his or her own background."[15]

According to Alves Nunes and Breno Pereira[16], in Japanese philosophy, knowledge is dynamic and created within social interactions between individuals and corporations. It is also humanistic, since it is essentially related to human action. Although it is an interactive process among individuals or between individuals and their environment, knowledge is strongly connected to the value system of individuals and the configuration of the network in which it is created. One refutation for this point is that, although there has been much research on Knowledge Management and Knowledge Sharing, this text considers Dan Paulin and Kaj Suneson's argument helpful in concluding that

"there is much overlap between the three terms knowledge transfer, Knowledge Sharing and knowledge, and such a lack of distinction is related mainly to the particular view and understanding of knowledge that is used for a particular interpretation."[17]

Finally, an underlying argument in favor of Knowledge Sharing in development cooperation is supported by Christian Freres, who defines it as an action though which knowledge, experiences and other tools and forms of knowledge are shared among people, communities, regions and countries.[18] In this way, the action of sharing is focused on knowledge as applied to

---

15   Paulin/Suneson 2015: 82.
16   Nunes/Pereira 2012.
17   Paulin/Suneson 2015: 89.
18   Freres 2013.

what works effectively. Knowledge and experience take center stage as being both the ingredients and products of current development processes. When such processes are applied between North and South, mutual learning occurs between stakeholders, with the North benefiting from knowledge provided by the South, and vice versa. It is this facility for enabling stakeholders from both North and South to grow from this sharing that makes knowledge and experience exchange a two-way process. Unlike before, knowledge and experiences are recognized as originating both in the North and in the South, and play a significant role in economic development and capacity building at the level of traditional and innovative industries.

At this point, it is necessary to allude to the World Bank's view of Knowledge Sharing, as a powerful way to transfer, replicate and extend what already works, to support countries interested in sharing and learning from their own experiences, including what not to do, and identifying practices worth adopting. Horizontal and inclusive associations in the global South are able to diversify and produce knowledge in ways that go beyond common patterns seen in industrialized countries, showcasing southern sources for development solutions.

Knowledge Sharing in policy and practice: boosting southern countries' potential for success

Based on the previous arguments, the purpose of this section is to analyse the links between Knowledge Sharing and development cooperation. Considering that this book is aimed at exploring the process of Knowledge Sharing in Latin America and the Caribbean, the author is interested in maintaining the perspective of international relations, enhanced global governance processes and the current situation of middle-income countries in a multipolar world.

Bringing the southern voice to the practice of Knowledge Sharing has taken time, and the role of emerging donors has been crucial in achieving this. Overwhelming evidence of this was visible at a workshop organized in 2011 by the Korean Development Institute (KDI) and the OECD Development Centre. One of the workshop's key messages focused on settling the difference between knowledge transfer or Knowledge Sharing, and Knowledge Management, where the first is unidirectional and the second implies bi-directional communication as well as internal generation of capacity. This set the basis for the next phase that is ownership. It was also concluded that effective Knowledge Sharing should be demand-based and imply an active interaction among peers.[19]

Even when the almost obsolete recipient-donor dichotomy is present, both development partners learn from each other, through the process of building capacity and exchanging knowledge. Based on available evidence that is the subject of high-level discussions, development banks and emerging donors have found that, as a result of the exchange, the capacity of a country to identify, formulate, implement and examine development solutions becomes more effective and efficient.[20]

The arguments here demonstrate that in the continuous search for development solutions by and for the global South, Knowledge Sharing is a natural fit when it comes to South-South debate and Triangular cooperation. Thus, local and regional knowledge finds its own place and use and, together with local and national resources, complements efforts by other stakeholders or traditional donors. To sum up, complementarity of North-South and South-South cooperation is acknowledged and supported by formal and innovative measures, and the outlook toward horizontal relations is increasingly optimistic.

Certainly, with the transition from the Millennium Development Goals to the Agenda 2030 for Development and its Sustainable Development Goals, the contemporary context provides evidence of significant demand for efforts by governments and social actors to generate good practices in Knowledge Sharing and experience exchange, and to foster collective measures to reach the targets and indicators. The key on this path is coordination at different levels and different stages, either public policies, sectoral public initiatives or regional and global networks. This directly involves North-South, South-South and triangular cooperation and the question is to enhance current practices and move toward innovative approaches, which will be successful as soon as they are aligned to public policies and governance processes.

Subsequently, as explained by Sheng Wang and Raymond Noe, new thinking defines Knowledge Sharing as the provision of task information and know-how to help others and to collaborate with others to solve problems, create new ideas, or implement policies and procedures.[21] This allows us to see how joint ventures, collective teams and co-production of

---

19   Freres 2013: 3.
20   Ibid.: 3.
21   Wang/Noe 2010.

knowledge would lead practices of development cooperation to horizontal dialogues and mutual learning processes.[22]

Table 1: Knowledge Sharing approaches to development

Unilateral	Knowledge seekers explore the existing universe of relevant knowledge codified in physical or virtual libraries and information repositories/databases.
Bilateral	Knowledge seekers share their respective experiences in a bilateral exchange. Often involves government-to-government cooperation programs.
Multilateral	Multiple knowledge seekers engage in a mutual, peer-to-peer exercise, exchanging their experiences and practices. Facilitated by international organisations.
North-South	Mainly finance coupled with technical co-operation. Has led to development outcomes benefitting millions of people in the developing world, but also revealed ways to address technical co-operation shortcomings, particularly through embedding demand-driven capacity development in national processes, including through development Knowledge Sharing.
South-South	Source of bilateral technical co-operation and development knowledge transfer, in many cases also accompanied by a significant transfer of financial resources.
Triangular Co-operation	The engagement of development assistance providers from both North and South in support of developing countries. Significant opportunities are emerging from this approach to promote learning on development experiences and to maximize resources, capacities and knowledge.

Source: Created by author based on World Bank 2015: 4-6.

---

22   To illustrate this, see Table 1.

Since the early nineties, multilateral organisations like OECD, Inter-American Development Bank or World Bank have usually combined diverse collaborative formats when supporting Knowledge Sharing platforms, either through policy networks, inclusive dialogues or peer learning. They also support and finance specific South-South cooperation projects in situ, mostly by government entities who act as knowledge providers or knowledge recipients. The inclusion of a broader private sector in southern countries has become more relevant, due to the wealth of knowledge that these actors usually manage, which commonly remains underutilized[23].

Certainly, these organisations have supported many development initiatives in the South to promote economic development and battle poverty. Nevertheless, the political factor is also at work in middle-income and low-income countries, specifically in the sense of candidates running on a platform of having access to multilateral funds. Undoubtedly, projects supported by these kinds of institutions achieve success in creating innovative experiences which can also be replicated. To reach this stage, the broader private sector in the South, including NGOs, universities, chambers of commerce and industry, foundations and research centers are currently on their way to attaining the degree of training necessary to be able to participate competitively.

From the perspective of triangular cooperation, Christian Freres and Nils-Sjard Schulz put forward the view that Knowledge Sharing constitutes "a third pillar" of development cooperation besides technical and economic cooperation[24]. Despite this, it cannot be said that there is a wide consensus about this: whereas some development actors try to advance straight forward to the enhancement of Knowledge Sharing, other actors still find the concept unclear, preferring to continue with traditional technical cooperation. Therefore, progress on Knowledge Sharing in Latin America and the Caribbean is neither complete nor homogeneous.

Although there has been relatively little research on Knowledge Sharing in Latin America, with existing reviews focusing on communitarian work and links with education systems, best practice consensus points to two types of knowledge related to development: knowledge about what and knowledge about how. The first refers to technical knowledge and ideas, currently the most prevalent focus, and the second to capacity building for knowledge production and application[25].

---

23   Costa 2015.
24   Freres/Schulz 2011; G20 2011.
25   Freres 2013.

Beyond South-South and triangular cooperation, another modality of organisation that has shown itself to be an effective platform for Knowledge Sharing is social and global networks, mentioned above, defined as those spaces of collective participation and horizontal collaboration where different inputs are gathered together to change the reality of a particular issue, developmental problem or social conduct. This certainly includes actors and activities of economic development, sectoral goods and services, and non-tangible goods (like knowledge itself).

In this regard, there are four mechanisms identified for sharing individual knowledge in an organisation:

Figure 1: Four Mechanisms for Sharing Individual Knowledge in an
              Organisation

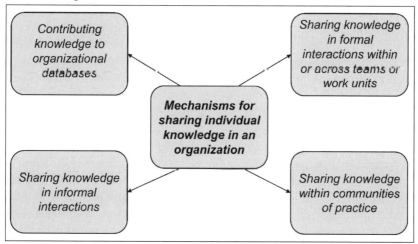

Source: Created by author, based on Vieira 2008; Bartol/Srivastava 2002.

This benefit can be obtained through international development cooperation, as well as global networks, by both North and South. Although this applies for an organisation, it is also applicable to development projects on a multi-actor basis.

After at least four decades of South-South Cooperation, its contribution to development is undeniable, as well as its role in complementing North-South cooperation. These dynamics, acknowledged throughout the Paris Accra process for the High-Level Agenda for Aid Effectiveness, have led the way to inclusive partnerships for development among public and private organisations. Knowledge Sharing has played a relevant role in this, enhanced still further by its core value of technical and scientific cooperation.

For Tubagus Choesni and Nils-Sjard Schulz, knowledge exchange entails the sharing of proven solutions developed and validated in a country or institution, which might be adapted and transferred to others in knowledge exchange, while practice-based expertise and successful solutions are shared to governments and institutions with scarce resources[26]. For that purpose, knowledge hubs emerge as the ideal figure for performing an enhanced form of Knowledge Sharing, as soon as coordination is reached between policy-makers and practitioners committed to effective development. Hubs could be found in public institutions, ministry line institutions, think tanks or regional networks, as can be seen in the different cases presented in this book. It will depend on the kind of knowledge that is needed and demanded by one side, the technicalities of its implementation, as well as where and for whom the information is produced.

In the same order of ideas, continuity is an aspect to be enhanced in good Knowledge Sharing practices, for which reason global networks or, even better, small steering committees on public projects present themselves as suitable for managing better coordination and small tasks in Knowledge Sharing. In other words, while national development cooperation agencies continue to dominate development activities, it is imprudent to ignore the impact of applying Knowledge Sharing practices on a smaller scale, such as projects run by specific networks and groups of actors, even when a larger impact is sought on national development as a whole.

As said by Tubagus Choesni and Nils-Sjard Schulz, knowledge hubs often represent the very best of a country's commitment and capacity for fighting poverty, achieved over decades of development processes, and are bound to become key pillars of a national development system based on solutions and practical experience[27]. It is appropriate to add here that, the stakeholders as the final beneficiaries are so important that they guarantee the sustainability and usage of the outcomes derived from the exchange.

Beyond beneficiaries, the issues of participation and how Knowledge Sharing can be carried out lead us to partnerships. On these, King and McGrath proposed that, before turning to the relationship between knowledge and partnership, it is necessary to consider some of the debates about partnership. They even specify that, rather than best practices, there are good practices. Instead of centering knowledge creation, they focus instead on local and social discovery. It is argued that resources should be

---

26   Choesni/Schulz 2011: 81.
27   Choesni/Schulz 2011.

directed at fostering information flows and supporting Southern capacity to create, acquire and apply knowledge.

South-South and triangular cooperation are excellent forms for disseminating Knowledge Sharing, but according to UNDP (United Nations Development Programme)[28], many countries have also expressed high expectations regarding the increasing useful and effective role of multilateral organisations as connectors and facilitators.[29]

Figure 2: Factors for high quality multilateral support

Source: Author adaptation of UNDP 2012: 46.

To achieve this, the presence of a broker, as previously mentioned, is required in the general management of South-South and triangular cooperation. The UN System considers that, given the development of the Latin American public institutions and their experience in knowledge and experience exchange, this should not be an issue.

---

28   UNDP 2012.
29   See Figure 2.

The potential is already there and there is a need for specific methodologies, financing platforms and mainstreaming a strategic approach for facilitating knowledge sources. The demand-driven approach becomes a tool taken for granted at the level of South-South cooperation in Latin America, whether it is embedded in the systems or not.

Having arrived at this point, it is necessary to indicate some constraints when implementing Knowledge Sharing processes. First, not all development actors have equal capacities for Knowledge Sharing or experience exchanges, nor to create development solutions. Institutional structures have different levels of reinforcing legal frameworks and political relations with the third sector to allow the creation of local and regional networks for development. As such, institutional coordination is a key issue, along with developing inclusive projects with strong dialogue among public and private actors, within an effective governance framework.

National development agencies in the South are not the only main actors in this field; smaller social and private actors conform a heterogeneous mosaic of potential hubs for Knowledge Sharing and creating development solutions. There is also a set of methodologies for doing so and an approach to work with. In the daily life of Knowledge Sharing at different levels and kinds of organisations, methodologies, approaches and sources of financial support are varied. There is no "one size fits all" recipe, and there is a gap between what is supported by multilateral and bilateral programs, and other groups of multi-actor networks, with mixed financial support and participation. Any generalisation could lead us to losing sight of other phenomena.

Several middle-income countries in Latin America have boosted important efforts to strengthen the institutional structure related to development cooperation, such as mainstreaming policies, establishing regulatory bodies, organisational reforms, staff training and country strategy papers, which all together set the foundation for facilitating Knowledge Sharing. Traditional donor agencies have been supporting these kinds of processes, as have multilateral institutions, with the aim of enhancing not only Knowledge Sharing, but development cooperation in general. As a finding, it can be said that one of the main objectives over the last ten years has been the mainstreaming of Knowledge Sharing into the rest of development issues, for both emerging donors and developing countries.

Furthermore, one benefit of this approach that aims to scale up Knowledge Sharing is innovation. Innovation might be understood as an inherent quality of networks that exchange experiences and knowledge, and also as one of their outcomes. Regarding innovation and development,

Glenda Kruss and Michael Gastrow argue that there is a strong causal interaction between capability-building and the growth in demand for, and supply of, technical and organisational innovation[30]. Therefore, taken together, this complex of skills, knowledge and innovation holds great potential for driving development, particularly in the context of developing countries[31].

Usually, literature about innovation has been related to production chains and economic activities; this is also true for research and development. In this case, Glenda Kruss and Michael Gastrow conclude that, despite evidence of the increasing importance of knowledge and innovation, there has been relatively little research done into the distribution and coordination of innovation and knowledge-intensive economic activities on a global scale – and what this might mean for economic development.[32]

Advantages and constraints of Knowledge Sharing in South-South cooperation

Emphasized here are the links between Knowledge Sharing and South-South and triangular cooperation, along with the evolved paradigm of development. Global development topics have been addressed by different development agendas. Bilateral and multilateral strategies have guided important efforts to elevate Knowledge Sharing to greater relevance. Non-government and combined global and regional networks have tapped the potential of Knowledge Sharing in different fields: public policies, economic development, value chains, science and technology, among others, fostering a mutual and continuous learning process.

Sooner or later, most development cooperation programs include activities related to Knowledge Sharing. Focusing on South-South and triangular cooperation, these activities have enjoyed a certain level of success, enabling horizontal relationships, a demand-driven approach and a potential stock of capacities and necessities for managing the right demand/supply cycle. Furthermore, the exchange of knowledge and experiences relies on what has worked effectively and what has not. In this regard, it is important to ensure a bidirectional flow of knowledge, considering more than one recipient.

---

30   Kruss/Gastrow 2012.
31   Grossman/Helpman 1991; teVelde 2005; Lorentzen 2009.
32   Kruss/Gastrow 2012.

Also of note is the importance of previous successful cooperation relationships, and geographical advantages, as well as a gradual transition away from the North being viewed as the source of all knowledge. When knowledge itself is assumed to be the main value, aimed at replicating an advantage either to upgrade a specific context or create development solutions, knowledge is equally valuable whether its origin is in the North or the South. Every country has something to provide and needs something from someone else.

While horizontality is pursued as part of many initiatives, it should not be taken for granted. Even amongst southern countries there is little conditionality or verticality when negotiating development issues and resources. In the case of triangular cooperation, ownership takes a special role in the process, thus, two processes of knowledge are involved: that provided by the development partners, and that which the recipient or beneficiary is building along the process of learning, while putting into operation the experiences, procedures, knowledge and ongoing reflections of the local people involved. In this regard, Christian Freres argues that the interrelationship among partners can produce new relevant knowledge for already embedded parties, as well as for third parties.[33]

Complementary to this, UNDP states that, moving towards good practices, knowledge and analysis on what works and what does not in South-South cooperation is still limited.[34] Despite this, lessons learned, criteria for quality, good practices, and the in-novation of modalities will all be critical for the South-South knowledge exchange to become a full-fledged, effective form of development cooperation[35].

Another essential point to discuss is the alignment of Knowledge Sharing with development targets, whether these are national, global or institutional. Most of the initiatives are designed to contribute toward solving specific issues; nevertheless, it is not feasible to show that all Knowledge Sharing is

---

33   Freres 2013.
34   UNDP 2012.
35   Regarding the current demand for collecting, monitoring and evaluating evidence on good practices in Knowledge Sharing, countries from Latin America and the Caribbean have advanced in the generation of systems and databases. There are successful experiences, most of them recorded by the Ibero-American Program (SEGIB), Economic Commission for Latin America and Caribbean (ECLAC), UNDP and Pan American Health Organization (PAHO). Some of them report implementation and dissemination of knowledge, whereas only a few can report impact evaluation. Regional integration platforms can also be included here, such as Caricom, Mercosur, Central American Integration System (SICA) and Unasur, whose yield cannot be registered.

designed to create evolution. A specific activity could be applied, for instance, to improve cooperation between Mexico and Japan in the field of aerospace knowledge. Or to enhance public transportation in Mexico City with the guidance of the local government of London. Both might contribute to development in the long term, nonetheless, there is no doubt that these experiences would imply a process of mutual learning and capacity building.

Notwithstanding, the 2030 Agenda for Development, while observance is assumed by all countries that ratified it, is not mandatory. Nevertheless, at local, national and regional levels, development actors are fostering initiatives to share experiences and technical knowledge, in order to contribute to development solutions, and report national or local progress. This represents a double-duty mission for governments in low and middle-income countries that have not yet successfully achieved the Millennium Development Goals; they are committed to implementing the Sustainable Development Goals according to the Agenda 2030, and to report achievements to the UN system in a race against time.

Additionally, southern countries have gradually adapted their economic models and political structure to the contemporary paradigm of development focused on human sustainable development, whereas current trends point to innovative demands within the paradigm of informational development.

The key aspect discussed here regards this change of paradigm, with informational development as a new form of social-techno-economic organisation built on a global level, which drives a new form of informational capitalism[36]. It is also characterized by a broad usage of digital information, technology and communication, promoting new forms of organisation in networks over all areas of social and economic life. Finally, the main question in current development policy concerns the relationship between informational development and human development.

Moreover, informational development enhances human life in two ways. First, through the technological dissemination of knowledge and the consequent broadening of network associations allowing regions and countries to get into global markets and globalisation on all terms. Secondly, by enabling widespread access to information and communication for producing, trading and delivering social services, including health and education.

It is possible to distinguish that informational development is substantially closer to Knowledge Sharing and experience exchange than human

---

36   Castells/Himanen 2016.

development. In this context, maintaining efforts in human development and sustainability is equally important. South-South and triangular cooperation have the potential to nurture both informational and human development with their common and innovative practices. These modalities of cooperation are integral to the global agenda for development or Agenda 2030, and the sustainable development goals.

Then again, know-how and human needs coincide in development solutions, by way of Knowledge Sharing, individual capacities and collective actions, as soon as they respond to public policies and national or local priorities. In the past, human needs were explored according to different perspectives. For instance, in the seventies, the International Labour Organisation considered five human needs including: basic goods (including food, housing and clothing), basic services (including education, health, access to water and transportation), participation, enjoyment of basic human rights, and productive employment. On the other hand, Len Doyal and Ian Dough determined universal needs as preconditions for social participation, adding self-determination, political freedom, national security, and cultural identity.[37]

To sum up, these approaches to human needs have represented relevant fields for the use of know-how, whether by international organisations, in North-South cooperation, or innovative formats such as global networks and local multi-actor initiatives. Certainly, Amartya Sen and Ahud Mal Abhiq's proposal on human development has also had an undeniable influence on the way development cooperation has evolved.

Final considerations

Originally, Knowledge Sharing, both as concept and process, was created by the North, thus, the basic premises and formats for bringing it into practice have shown a mostly Northern mind-set. Nevertheless, the path followed over the last fifteen years and the South's participation in its construction have demonstrated that technical cooperation and capacity building have brought different characteristics and processes to southern countries.

More importantly, the practice of Knowledge Sharing in the South has shown that several actors have great potential to evolve in many fields of development: not only in science and technology, but also in public policy,

---

37   Doyal/Dough 1991.

economics and local development. Complementary to this, beyond the fields of practice, the core value of Knowledge Sharing in the North and especially in the South, is its proven ability to promote horizontality, ownership and self-reliance, which could be translated into sustainable practices and inclusive partnerships.

Hence, although initially used in the North, Knowledge Sharing has established original roots and self-development in the South, within Southern countries and among development actors, independently of their nature. Also, it has been seen that, with proper seed capital and guidance, development actors in the South can formulate and perform development projects with success. There are still many challenges in gathering diversified financial sources, creating stronger participatory structures, consolidating methodologies for effectiveness, and building a strategic view of development cooperation. In brief, there is no single way to generate Knowledge Sharing; each case is different according to where we are standing, the nature of the institutions involved, the legal framework and the capacities of the participants.

Digital platforms have been an excellent instrument for creating Knowledge Sharing programs, when development partners find ways to avoid relying on them too heavily, fostering knowledge and experience as the core value of the action. In the beginning, reliance on digital platforms received the support of national governments in both donor and developing partner countries; however, this has changed and many groups and networks have learnt to provide a range resources within cost-sharing frameworks.

In short, the mere existence of multipolar projects and networks could be considered a success, given that fifteen years ago they were by no means inevitable. Nowadays, they are growing rapidly with a core focus on knowledge, how to share it and, even more importantly, keeping its outcomes sustainable and effective in the long term, providing continuity to development solutions achieved through the Knowledge Sharing experience. Equally important are networks and collective multi-actor projects, as effective platforms for disseminating and creating more knowledge, and keeping it available for different communities of practice, once they establish a code of conduct that enshrines the principles of equity and participation.

Regarding the OECD classification of Knowledge Sharing, and in addition to common practices in Latin American countries, it is the author's wish to emphasize the rise and usefulness of social relations and epistemic communities through networks and cooperation, either in bilateral relations or within multipolar formats. This kind of practice has gradually become more common in a broad range of environments, such as government, local and social development, urban development, biodiversity or economic-productive. Knowledge Sharing, in this regard, exists beyond educational environments and formal educational spaces. These structures have been surpassed by technology and participatory systems, including non-hierarchical groups, shared management, participatory groups and workshops.

Despite limited evidence, it is possible to affirm that effective Knowledge Management and Knowledge Sharing have administrative, budgetary and staff constraints. For instance, an adverse environment would jeopardize a project of social and urban planning; negotiating with local authorities, commonly driven by corruption and patronage, would create a power imbalance in the middle of the project. Additionally, technical modernisation processes and a social re-education program would require a large amount of investment, organisation, negotiation, cutting-edge technology, staff training and procedural handbooks.

Depending upon the case, the country and the field of execution, Knowledge Sharing can come into play and leverage several fields of development. Some of them would demand technical capabilities, whereas other would demand specialized training. In the long term, technological development would have strong leverage, despite a lower social impact in the short term, and the authentic social impact would remain within specialized capabilities, both on an individual and institutional level. When it is effective, Knowledge Sharing can accelerate learning processes on the side of beneficiaries, as well as the rest of the stakeholders.

Bibliography

Ayala Martínez, Citlali/Müller, Ulrich (2014): Implementation, Ownership, Cooperation as Challenges of Global Governance, in: Lázaro Rüther, Lena/Ayala Martínez, Citlali/Müller, Ulrich (eds.): Global Funds and Networks. Narrowing the Gap between Global Policies and National Implementation, Nomos, Baden-Baden, pp. 27-62.

Bartol, Kathryn M./Srivastava, Abhishek (2002): Encouraging Knowledge Sharing: The Role of Organisational Reward Systems, Journal of Leadership and Organisational Studies, Vol. 9(1), pp. 64–77.

Castells, Manuel/Himanen, Pekka (eds.) (2016): Reconceptualización del desarrollo en la era global de la información, Fondo de Cultura Económica, Santiago de Chile.

Choesni, Tubagus/Schulz, Nils-Sjard (2011): Knowledge Hubs – Progress in Practice since the Bali Communiqué, in: Kato, Hiroshi/Honda, Shunichiro (eds.): Tackling Global Challenges through Triangular Cooperation, Japan International Cooperation Agency Research Institute, Tokyo, pp. 81-100.

Costa Vazquez, Karin (2015): South-South Knowledge Transfer: Transferring Knowledge and building capacity in Latin America and the Caribbean. Program Report, Multilateral Investment Fund, Washington, January 2015.

Doyal, Len/Dough, Ian (1991): A Theory of Human Need, London, Macmillan.

Freres, Christian (2013): El intercambio de conocimientos en la cooperación triangular en América Latina y el Caribe, CEPEI, Bogotá.

Freres, Christian/Schulz, Nils-Sjard (2011): Emerging Lessons on Institutionalizing Country-Led Knowledge Sharing - G20 Issues Paper, World Bank Institute.

King, Kevin/McGrath, Simon (2004): Knowledge-based aid. A four agency comparative study, International Journal of Education Development, Vol. 24(2), pp. 167-181.

Kruss, Glenda/Gastrow, Michael (2012): Global innovation networks, human capital, and development, Innovation and Development, Vol. 2(2), pp. 205-208. Accessible under: http://dx.doi.org/10.1080/2157930X.2012.724885 (11.08.2017).

Lázaro Rüther, Lena/Ayala Martínez, Citlali/Müller, Ulrich (eds.) (2014): Global Funds and Networks. Narrowing the Gap between Global Policies and National Implementation, Nomos, Baden-Baden.

Leutner, Jana/Müller, Ulrich (2010): Ownership in Practice, in: Frenken, Sarah/Müller, Ulrich (eds.): Ownership and Political Steering in Developing Countries, Nomos, Baden-Baden, pp. 47-59.

Maddison, Angus (1965): Foreign Skills and Technical Assistance in Economic Development, OECD Development Centre, Paris.

Nunes Alves, Juliano/Pereira Diniz, Breno Augusto (2012): Knowledge Sharing in horizontal networks. The proposition of a framework, Pensamiento y Gestión, No. 33, pp. 39-66.

Parker Rosell, Hèctor Carlos (2007): Construcción de redes de conocimiento. Revista del Centro de Investigación, Universidad La Salle, Mexico, Vol. 7(27), pp. 93-119.

Paulin, Dan/Suneson, Kaj (2015): Knowledge Transfer, Knowledge Sharing and Knowledge Barriers – Three Blurry Terms in KM, Online Journal of Applied Knowledge Management, International Institute for Applied Knowledge Management, Vol. 3(1), pp. 81-91.

UNDP (United Nations Development Programme) (2012): Mapping Multilateral Support to South-South Cooperation in Latin America and the Caribbean. Towards Collaborative Approaches, UNDP, Panama.

Vieira Marques, Dulce/Cardoso, Leonor/Zappalá, Salvatore (2008): Comportamento Organizacional e Gestão, Knowledge Sharing networks and performance, Vol. 14(2), pp. 161-192.

Wang, Sheng/Noe, Raymond A. (2010): Knowledge sharing. A review and directions for future research, Human Resource Management Review, Vol 20(2), pp. 115-131.

Wiedenhof, Caroline/Molenaar, Henk (2006): One never knows. Research policy and Knowledge Management in Dutch development cooperation, Knowledge Management for Development Journal, Vol. 2(3), pp. 5-18.

World Bank (2015): Scaling up Knowledge Sharing for development. A working paper for the G-20 development working group, Pillar 9, World Bank Group, Washington, D.C. Accessible under: http://documents.worldbank.org/curated/en/4291114681 88931035/Scaling-up-knowledge-sharing-for-development-a-working-paper-for-the-G-20-development-working-group-pillar-nine (11.08.2017).

Making a Difference: Competences for Knowledge Sharing

Ulrich Müller[1]

"Let yourself be built up as living stones to the spiritual house"[2]

Today's changing world needs new formats for cooperation. The distinction between "us" and "them"[3] is no longer helpful when considering new, global challenges that can only be faced together. Meanwhile, recent tendencies toward highlighting differences and building walls between countries and continents express an increasing uncertainty about the future. While thinking and acting globally appears to be a need, the new world is not yet shaping sufficiently for generally creating confidence, optimism and a vision of a better life. Legacies of the past are strong and entrenched within institutions and organisations. The discourse around new forms of cooperation is too often limited to mere rhetoric, while practices remain the same. If Knowledge Sharing is one way toward a new future for cooperation - as suggested by Sustainable Development Goal (SDG) 17, "Strengthen the means of implementation and revitalize the global partnership for sustainable development"[4] – how can it mark a difference?

There are good reasons why Knowledge Sharing has been the subject of increasing interest in the area of international development cooperation, because it corresponds with many of the lessons learnt over past decades, as will be pointed out in the first part of this article. But there are also reasons why it is applied less than could be expected. Not everything that is called

---

1   Many thanks to Bernd Krewer and Balthas Seibold for their generous input toward the creation of this article.
2   It is one of the characteristics of Knowledge Sharing that instead of authors searching for messages, things are rather working the other way round: messages find people who – beyond intention and dogma – let them flow and develop. This has also been the case with this quote from the first letter of Peter, chapter 5, verse 2, that – as will be seen - surprisingly provided the structure for the main part of this article.
3   Meadows 2014.
4   United Nations 2015.

Knowledge Sharing meets the expectations of collaboration among equals and co-creation.

Knowledge Sharing is demanding because it means more than just the application of a new formula that can be transmitted easily and then replicated on a massive scale. It requires a change of attitude and the ability to link existing knowledge with that brought in by new partners, to step back and self-reflect, and to derive the "creative impulse from otherness"[5] that means learning through others. In the second part of the article these requirements are discussed in terms of their role in shaping four fields of competence that make up the spirit – or the art – of Knowledge Sharing: personal competence, subject area competence, social competence and methods competence[6]. Knowledge Sharing is generally conceived as a process between persons who may develop these competences. At the same time, they are embedded in organisations and societies, within which they develop their competences and apply the knowledge shared. Hence the context of organisations and societies can be more or less favorable for Knowledge Sharing. The corresponding requirements at organisational and society level will therefore also be discussed in the second part. The argument will further be enriched with references to cases from Latin America and the Caribbean.

Finally, the conclusion places Knowledge Sharing in the context of current trends in international development cooperation, pointing out that efforts to meet the requirements of Knowledge Sharing are timely, worthwhile and necessary as a means to face increasingly complex global development challenges.

Knowledge Sharing in Development Cooperation

Traditional concepts of development cooperation depart from the idea that developing countries are largely lacking in two things that must be transferred to them by developed countries: finance and knowledge[7]. The corresponding instruments are the provision of grants and loans on one hand and knowledge transfer on the other. The idea of knowledge transfer parted as

---

5   Krewer/Uhlmann 2015: 17.
6   Ibid.: 13.
7   Schätzl 1986: 82.

most classical didactical approaches from the "primacy of content"[8] and a linear transmission from experts to learners, from master to novice.

Further theoretical reflection and learning from experience in development cooperation exposed the shortfalls in the simplistic idea of development as merely a transfer of financing and knowledge. This perspective has received criticism from many different angles; nevertheless, the initial uni-directional transfer models continue to persist into the present.

In the 1960s and 70s, with important input from Latin America, dependency theory argued that underdevelopment is a consequence of power relations and structural disadvantages in the global economy. From that point of view, it is an over-involvement in a long history of one-sided relations and dependencies, a "centuries-long participation in the process of world capitalist development"[9] that has to be overcome, rather than an under-involvement in development processes.

Apart from colonial and neo-colonial power dynamics, one of the main factors in these one-sided relationships is the high concentration of innovation "in large cities with large and diversified labour pools, mixed and open cultures which favour the communication of new information, fluid financing facilities, heavy endowments of infra-structural capital and potent educational and research institutions"[10]. While good ideas may emerge anywhere, the processes of sorting them out, then improving and creating products, can only occur where top knowledge and resources converge and Knowledge Sharing processes can take place most easily.

Starting in the 1970s and 80s, it has been increasingly acknowledged that development cannot be brought from abroad but has to come from within a society. Developing countries have to be agents of their own development. Consequently, the role of external partners is not the mere transfer of financing and knowledge, but also the strengthening of self-help capacities and an approach of "empowerment" that "places the emphasis on autonomy in the decision-making of territorially-organized communities, local self-reliance (but not autarchy), direct (participatory) democracy, and experimental social learning"[11].

---

8   Krewer/ Uhlmann 2015: 25.
9   Frank 1969: 7.
10   Lasuén 1973: 178, based on Thompson 1965.
11   Friedmann 1992: vii.

In the aid effectiveness debate of the 2000s, this is reflected in the principle of ownership[12] that "can be defined as the idea that societies as well as individuals assume the responsibility for their own development"[13]. As the authors further point out, "the main problem of development is how actors and actions are brought together"[14]. In consequence, the issue is not the availability of funds and knowledge but how these are used for development purposes. There is a gap[15] between discourse and practice, strategy and implementation, knowledge and learning, financial resources and their adequate use[16]. This gap has to be overcome by combining different competences in technical, political and managerial fields; combinations which will rarely be found in individuals, but rather require the collaboration of several actors.[17]

Another strand of recent publications has analysed development from a historical perspective[18]. All three books come to the conclusion that "politics and institutions are the crucial determinants of development outcomes"[19]. Institutions are formed and shaped through "the relation between what agents can do and do do, on the one hand, and the constraints and opportunities of the structures in which they operate, on the other hand"[20]. Therefore

> "the most demanding contemporary challenge … is how to understand, promote and advance the local politics that will shape the institutions that in turn will facilitate not only sustainable growth, but inclusive growth, transformation and social development, as well as political stability"[21].

The connection with the argument in the previous paragraph is striking: Development does not depend on the availability of finance and knowledge,

---

12 In the Paris Declaration from 2005 ownership is the first of five principles for effective development cooperation. The others are alignment (2), harmonisation (3), managing for results (4) and mutual accountability (5).
13 Leutner/Müller 2010: 48.
14 Ibid.: 54.
15 On the idea of the "gap" in development cooperation see Ayala Martínez/Müller 2014: 45ff.
16 Müller/Kenngott 2009: 28; Leutner/Müller 2010: 54.
17 Regarding the practical implications of this understanding of development see GIZ 2015.
18 North et al. 2009, Fukuyama 2011, Acemoglu/Robinson 2012.
19 Laws/Leftwich 2012: 20.
20 Ibid.: 23.
21 Ibid.: 25.

but on the ability of different actors with different competences to interact and share their respective knowledge and resources.

Also, from the learning perspective, the idea of a linear transmission of content has been left behind. Teaching today "is conceptualized as a joint process built by the teacher and learners, in which complex, differentiated learning incentives are 'co-constructed', challenging people to learn"[22]. This draws the attention to "the learner's inner process, the context of learning and the people with whom and from whom learning takes place"[23], the step-by-step and interrelated progression of cognitive, motivational and affective elements or in other words "knowledge, ability and attitude"[24].

All these findings somehow converge in the concept of Knowledge Sharing. Knowledge Sharing is an open and creative way to deal with knowledge in international development cooperation. Persons, organisations and societies learn from each other in order to strengthen their capacity for sustainable development. Knowledge Sharing leads towards new cooperation dynamics in which all partners involved are ready to share with and learn from others. Therefore, it opens perspectives for innovation and co-creation. In Knowledge Sharing all partners are experts and develop a new understanding – one that can only be achieved by using and combining existing knowledge from different sources in order to create new solutions for different contexts.

Requirements for Knowledge Sharing

When people meet and exchange information, Knowledge Sharing does not simply appear or function automatically. It requires persons competent in the knowledge, abilities and attitudes that allow Knowledge Sharing, as well as an organisational and societal setting that establishes positive conditions for joint learning and co-creation. Knowledge Sharing refers to a quality and efficiency of communication that consists of four main elements:

- committed and open partners ready to learn and to share (self-reflection and "we"-reflection, together with curiosity and willingness to change);

---

22   Krewer/Uhlmann 2015: 26.
23   Ibid.: 26.
24   Ibid.: 15.

- a joint view on the problem to which the shared knowledge is to be applied, using a results- and implementation-oriented approach (problem reflection)
- trusting relationships among equal partners and a mutual translation of knowledge to the language of the partners (reflection on communication and cooperation)
- formats and facilitation appropriate to settings and contexts, allowing processes of co-creation and open innovation (methods reflection).

With regard to persons that engage in Knowledge Sharing, these requirements correspond with the four fields that form the competence model devised by GIZ's (Gesellschaft für Internationale Zusammenarbeit) Academy for International Cooperation[25]: (1) personal competence, (2) subject area competence, (3) social competence and (4) methods competence[26]. These four fields of competence will be discussed further on, with regard to their relevance to the spirit or the art of Knowledge Sharing. While the idea of competences primarily refers to the level of persons, the way in which they relate with organisations and society will also be considered. Personal learning has to materialize in organisational and societal processes. There are many options as to how this can be made possible, be it through focusing on decision makers as in the Alliance for Financial Inclusion[27] or by connecting Knowledge Sharing to approaches of institutional twinning as in the case of the National Auditing Authorities of Chile and Peru[28]. Attention will also be drawn to the conditions in organisations and societies that provide an enabling setting for persons to engage in Knowledge Sharing with the necessary freedom and openness.

---

25   See Figure 1.
26   The same elements are also reflected more poetically in this article's opening quote: "Let yourself (personal competence) be built up (subject area competence) as living stones (social competence) to the spiritual house (methods competence)."
27   See Box 1.
28   See Box 3.

Figure 1: The Fields of Competence Model

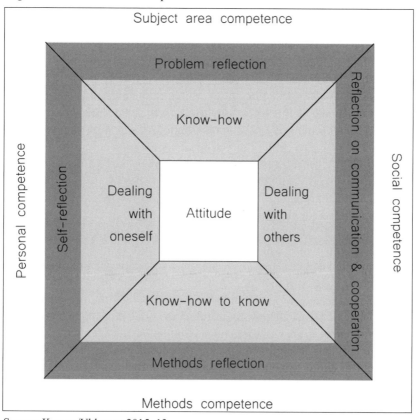

Source: Krewer/Uhlmann 2015: 13.

Personal competence

In his book on improvisation and the theatre, Keith Johnstone starts with an interesting example of self-reflection that he calls "notes on myself"[29]. Trying "to be clever in everything," he experienced that he became "reluctant to attempt anything for fear of failure" because "everything had to be corrected and brought into line"[30]. But then he noticed "how warped many people of great intelligence are" and "began to value people for their actions,

---

29   Johnstone 1981: 17.
30   Ibid.: 17.

rather than their thoughts"[31]. Nevertheless, he did not confuse this insight with a call to action. Inspired by his art teacher, Keith Johnstone instead found truth in Taoist ideas:

> "I take no action and the people are transformed of themselves; I prefer stillness and the people are rectified on themselves; I'm not meddlesome and the people prosper of themselves. I am free from desire and the people of themselves become simple like the uncarved block"[32].

Being a teacher himself later, he tells students "that they mustn't try to control the future, or to 'win'; and that they're to have an empty head and just watch"[33].

It is this kind of self- and other-reflection that leads to the practice of Knowledge Sharing and that is summarized in the two first words of the initial quote in this article: "let yourself ...." Allowing oneself to be surprised, moved and inspired from others and reflecting critically on own experiences and truths is the way of a "realistic, step-by-step progression towards the competences that international cooperation needs today: co-creative minds capable of shaping ownership as well as alignment with the development strategies of partners"[34].

Acting in such a way goes against what appears to be the normal practice in the world of today. We are accustomed to controlling, categorizing and operationalizing. We have learned that complexity has to be reduced in order to be able to act, that activities must be disclosed in steps that rationally nourish one another, and that a distinction has to be made between what is right and wrong. Taking these ideas as a starting point, the often limited availability of knowledge, its fragmentation and the ambiguity of meaning when changing from one context to another is generally considered as a nuisance, something that has to be overcome and will not exist anymore in the ideal world of constantly available, complete and undoubted knowledge. Accordingly, solution packages and institutionalized procedures are sought, as well as documented experiences, catalogues, lists, toolboxes, rules and standards, while what is often needed is an attitude of curiosity.

The two words "let yourself ..." invite the opposite: to loosen control, accept ambiguities as an opportunity and take fragmentation as a chance to communicate, appreciate and look in the other for what is lacking in oneself. This is the idea behind many open source processes. Intellectual property is

---

31   Ibid.: 18.
32   Ibid.: 20.
33   Ibid.: 32.
34   Krewer/Uhlmann 2015: 17.

not erected as a hurdle for collaboration, and as-yet unfinalized ideas are put on the market place of inspiration and creativity and allowed to be changed, split and rebuilt, decontextualized and reshaped. Thus, learning is "organized in peer production based on open licensing and a decentralized, collaborative and non-proprietary process of global knowledge co-creation"[35].

This is not an easy path because it questions how knowledge has been commonly dealt with in the past. Professionalism and standards for academic work have been created. Figures are rather trusted than feelings. The intellectual effort of digging deep into topics and creating new ideas and solutions is remunerated by guaranteeing intellectual property rights. All these systems are in place and have proven to be successful. Nevertheless, they are not necessarily helpful when it comes to Knowledge Sharing. Thus, many think that Knowledge Sharing may be a nice idea, but has no place in real life or at best could be seen as an interesting footnote to the dominant and well-founded practices of protected knowledge. What is needed instead is a new understanding of joint authorship.

Nevertheless, reality is not as bleak as these reflections suggest. Many have lived on some occasion the kind of freedom and openness that lies in Knowledge Sharing. Often new ideas and innovations have surprisingly been achieved that way. It proves to be highly liberating to go beyond control and perfection, with the quest for the impossible being indispensable when pragmatism and realism alone fail to bring forward the necessary answer. Freedom and openness allow an organic, rather than an encyclopedic way of dealing with knowledge that is often closer to reality than abstractions and generalisations. It has been increasingly acknowledged that knowledge is always contextual and cannot be owned by experts, although their broad experience and deep thoughts into specific matters are valuable. Awareness of one's own values, abilities and experiences is connected with an increasing capacity for thinking and understanding the other. Knowledge Sharing therefore asks for a categorical shift in ways of thinking and acting. In this context, the creation of new cooperation agencies in emerging countries offers an interesting new perspective. The way they connect with others is not unidirectional but two-sided: they coordinate incoming and outgoing cooperation. Hence, there is a lot of room for rethinking the role of experts and organisations in development cooperation in projects between traditional donors and these new agencies, such as the Mexican-German

---

35   Seibold 2014: 2.

project for the strengthening of the Mexican Cooperation Agency, AMEX-CID (Agencia Mexicana de Cooperación Internacional para el Desarrollo).

Nonetheless "let yourself…" does not mean to move from a dogma of order and control to a new dogma of openness and freedom, where no standard is allowed anymore, all checklists are rejected and it is forbidden to suggest that something might be wrong. This would be as one-sided and repressive than the intent to categorize and manage everything. "Let yourself…" means to accept that different ways are possible and all of them are valuable, although not all may finally prove to be good. Knowledge Sharing in that way reconciles standards and norms, lists and tools with the exception from the rule and may even be helpful in creating a broader identification with norms and standards than any application of force would do. Negotiating between different stakeholders with different levels of power, for instance in the multi-stakeholder groups of the Extractive Industries Transparency Initiative (EITI), may be a long process, but it is "difficult to come up with feasible alternatives"[36].

Finally, "let yourself …" also means allowing for failure. It has become commonplace to demand that there should be more communication about failures than about success stories because there is so much to be learned from failure. Nevertheless, it is of little help to demand the openness to talk about failures. It is much more promising to create spaces of mutual trust where the risk of admitting failures can be diminished. In that sense "let yourself …" in Knowledge Sharing always means also to "let the other."

Subject area competence

In spite of its notion of freedom and openness and its power to question control of knowledge and the quest for perfect solutions, Knowledge Sharing is not unintentional. Having a common goal and a shared understanding of the problems of focus is one of the success factors of Knowledge Sharing that have been formulated in such contexts as the Alliance for Financial Inclusion (AFI)[37]. Knowledge Sharing has to be directed and change-oriented. That is the only way to justify the effort and to seriously recognize the time and resources invested by the partners. Knowledge Sharing will never be embraced by the self-sufficient.

---

36   Leutner/Rösch 2014: 217.
37   See Box 1; Hannig et al. 2015.

Box 1: The Alliance for Financial Inclusion

The global peer-learning and knowledge-sharing network Alliance for Financial Inclusion (AFI) was officially launched in September 2009. Members are policymakers from 119 Central Banks and key national financial regulators from 95 developing and emerging countries[38]. What brings them together is the desire to increase financial inclusion of poor people, since an estimated 2.5 billion people, most of them from Africa, Asia, Latin America and the Middle East, lack access to formal financial services such as savings accounts, insurance or payment systems[39].

In 2006, on the initiative of the Bill & Melinda Gates Foundation and German Development Cooperation, GIZ, a core group of opinion leaders from developing countries, mainly governors and deputy governors of Central Banks, met together and started an open dialogue on approaches to promote financial inclusion. Step by step they decided on the topics and working mechanisms of the emerging member-driven network. The policy areas AFI currently supports are[40]:

- Balancing Inclusion, Integrity and Stability,
- Consumer Empowerment and Market Conduct,
- Digital Financial Services,
- Financial Inclusion Strategy,
- Measuring Financial Inclusion,
- Small and Medium Enterprise Finance,
- Other financial inclusion policies.

Apart from joint learning, the network influences Agenda Setting at the G20 level and creates joint commitments like the Maya Declaration of 2011, which forms the "first global and measurable set of commitments to financial inclusion"[41]. Other services offered by the network are thematic working groups and platforms, grants for Knowledge Sharing and policy support and annual meetings of members and external partners (Global Policy Forum, GPF).

---

38   Figures as of June 2016.
39   Hannig et al. 2014: 200.
40   Hannig et al. 2015: 6.
41   Ibid.: 9.

AFI's affairs are conducted by a Steering Committee. The first Steering Committee was formed by the Central Banks of Kenya, the Philippines and Thailand as well as Mexico's National Banking and Securities Commission. They were later joined by the Banking and Ensurance Supervisory Agency of Peru and the Central Bank of Nigeria. Later Kenya, Mexico and Thailand were replaced by the Central Banks of Tanzania and Indonesia and the Banking Supervisory Agency of Guatemala[42]. The Steering Committee's decisions are implemented by AFI's Management Unit (MU), first based in Bangkok and later moved to Kuala Lumpur. The MU is overseen by GIZ and provides professional management, monitoring & evaluation (M&E) and member relations.

According to AFI's internal monitoring data from June 2016, more than 190 policy improvements and reforms have been directly supported since 2009. On the 27th of January, 2016, AFI was established as a permanent international organisation based in Malaysia, and by June 2016 it was receiving membership fees from 63 institutions[43].

The foundation of Knowledge Sharing in subject area competence calls for making the self and professional identities compatible. Openness and the ability to relax control required at the personal competence level must go hand in hand with a high subject area competence. Although it has to be acknowledged that there is no such thing as complete and un-fragmented knowledge, "high quality information" is nevertheless needed for successful strategic development management[44].

This also means that Knowledge Sharing should not be considered as the one and only answer to any kind of problem. If you know what to do and have the means to do it, why look for somebody else with whom to share and partner? Nevertheless, there are other challenges where neither goals nor methods are known[45]. It is with these that it can be worthwhile to engage partners who bring in additional elements, experiences and knowledge.

---

42   Ibid.: 7.
43   Ambadar 2016.
44   Mummert/Mummert 2010: 37.
45   See Figure 2.

Figure 2: Action and Ambiguity

	Objectives: clear, uncontroversial	Objectives: unclear, controversial
Method and technology: clear, uncontroversial	Calculation Bureaucracy Hierarchy	Bargaining Represen- tation Pluralism
Method and technology: unclear, controversial	Judgment Collegium Professionalism	Arguing Network Politics

Source: Ayala/Müller 2014 based on Jann 2009.

In the quote at the beginning of this article, subject area competence relates to the words "be built up." The goal of Knowledge Sharing is a development goal, where something new is constructed among partners. Accordingly, involvement by the partners goes beyond providing data and figures to bring subject area competence into a joint process together with partners.

It should also be acknowledged that different forms of subject area competence are possible. Subjects do not exist in an original objective truth outside of human beings but exist within them, through their relationships with the world[46]. Experts are not in a neutral position towards their area of expertise, and those who experience the area in daily life are also experts, whether or not they have studied it in an academic context. What is needed is an understanding that professional expertise is only one way to develop new solutions. It should be combined with other worldviews and perspectives of "everyday users." An example of this approach is the recognition of farmers' knowledge in agricultural extension work[47].

---

46   Freire 1973: 89.
47   See Box 2; See also the contribution by Horacio Rodriguez in this book.

Box 2: Farmer First

In 1989 Robert Chambers, together with Lori Ann Thrupp and Arnold Pacey, in their book Farmer First stressed "the importance of giving priority to farmers' agendas and knowledge" against the usual "transfer of technology thinking and action, where 'we' determine priorities, generate technologies and then transfer them to farmers, and where farmers' participation is limited to adoption"[48]. The range of "practical approaches and methods for farmer participation in research" and the "implications for outsiders' roles and for institutions"[49] can be seen as an early case study in Knowledge Sharing that already showed the difficulties of putting such an approach into practice. As Robert Chambers points out: "All too easily, the farmer-first label and the rhetoric of participation have been adopted without the substance"[50].

When brought to Latin America, the farmer-first approach entered into a situation of knowledge conflict expressed by Andean peasants in Peru in the following way: "We are losing our ancestral knowledge, because the technicians only believe in science and cannot read the sky"[51]. The conflict had already entered the communities, where different groups debated over the use of traditional or modern knowledge, as Salas[52] paraphrases a dialogue in a rural village in Peru:

> "The young one says: 'Grandpas, how do you still believe in all this nonsense. You should grow potatoes using chemical fertilizers. Until when will you be harvesting these tiny potatoes? Now that science has advanced you could do much better.' The elders answer, 'Sons, you are real fools, the scientific potato only brings more diseases, the high yielding varieties are poisonous for mother earth and for you. Look at us, we are old but healthy because we don't eat the improved varieties which are treated with chemicals.'"

Within this context interesting experiences emerged that "explicitly" avoided "using standardized methods and 'recipes' for developing participatory tools and exercises"[53]. Instead, local people were encouraged "to adapt methods and innovate, adjusting approaches to local conditions and interests" so that they were able to develop "understanding and 'own-

---

48   Chambers 1994: xiii.
49   Ibid.: xiii.
50   Ibid.: xiii.
51   Salas 1994: 57.
52   Ibid.: 67.
53   Thrupp et al. 1994: 172.

ership' of the methods" thus making the approach "compatible with Andean perceptions of nature, causality and time"[54]. The recognition of traditional knowledge and cultural practices was introduced as a principle for instruments of rural development such as land use planning[55]. Experience also showed the benefit of involvement by "representatives from many interest groups, classes, ages and both genders"[56] and the inclusion of "not only local people and NGOs, but also representatives of public institutions and/or private sector who are stakeholders in the main issues under consideration"[57] with the objective of linking participatory initiatives with policy decisions in order to scale up effects to larger areas and more people.

Social Competence

Getting involved with others requires social competence, the ability to reflect on communication and cooperation and to understand that "learning always takes place 'through' the 'other' … 'Novelty' and 'otherness' provide the inspiration to learn. Sensing a disparity from oneself (often represented by people) and having to adopt a position towards it sets in train a learning process for the learner"[58].

An important factor in this context is the ability to promote improbable encounters[59]. In groups whose members have different experiences and points of view, there is high potential for the entire group to be enriched when these are shared. There is an understandable tendency to seek out persons with similar experiences and viewpoints. But what feels good does not always show good results. On the other hand, engaging with persons, organisations and societies of different cultures creates the need for building trust first and understanding what the other means. The intercultural competence required is not only a matter of people coming from different parts of the world. It begins between organisations from different cultures, be-

---

54   Ibid.: 172.
55   Müller 1999: 14
56   Thrupp et al. 1994: 173.
57   Ibid.: 176.
58   Krewer/Uhlmann 2015: 15.
59   Ziemer 2015.

tween persons with different professional backgrounds, e.g. artists and law-yers, practitioners and academics, implementers and politicians. This also means that current assumptions about cultural proximity and distance are less important than the overall capacity to work interculturally[60]. Prejudice is a common problem, but there is also much to be gained when the improb-able encounter works. The real challenge is to deal competently with cul-tural diversity – wherever it comes from – and to use it jointly for creating new habits, solutions and attitudes.

Nevertheless, the idea of improbable encounters should not be inter-preted to mean that Knowledge Sharing always has to be multi-stakeholder. There is also a high potential to build within peer-to-peer contexts. Here understanding is easier, a common language can be found more quickly and it is possible to reach points where the real problems and failures can be addressed. The choice between multi-stakeholder and peer-to-peer Knowledge Sharing depends on the challenges and goals of Knowledge Sharing and on the composition of the initial group. Organically, case by case, group constellations and joint procedures must be found that truly promise the ability to build together.

In the initial quote in this article, social competence coincides with the words "… as living stones…" The idea of living stones is important to un-derstanding Knowledge Sharing for two reasons. First, there is a notion of equality on the level of individual attitude as well as in the relationship be-tween organisations and societies. All group members are useful stones, forming a part of what is built. No single one is better or more useful than the others, and all are needed together. There is no single architect, rather all those involved are sharing the process of building and finding out what fits and what is useful. In order to achieve this, the 'stones' must be in con-tact with one another; this contact is always unique and specific, but at the same time part of the same building. In Knowledge Sharing, there is contact between persons, but these are part of a greater and overarching process, like in the peer-production of open source software where many parts of the code later form a computer program able to perform complex tasks[61].

To achieve equality is not easy. Partners in Knowledge Sharing always differ, even in peer-to-peer encounters, in terms of the status and power they hold. In AFI, for instance, all members are central bankers and from finan-cial control institutions. All occupy high level, important posts within their organisations. But nevertheless, some come from big countries while others

---

60   Müller/Knodt 2012: 145.
61   Raymond 2000.

come from small countries. There are also differences in knowledge and training that may lead to a higher or lower status among members. And finally, there are founding members and there are newer members. Equality in Knowledge Sharing is something that partners must decide actively: 'I want to deal with all partners on equal terms.' "Liberating action necessarily involves a moment of perception and volition"[62]. There is one helpful factor for equality: Knowledge Sharing has no hierarchy. It is a voluntary exchange. Whoever does not feel welcome or well-treated may withdraw.

The other aspect relates to the word 'living.' Knowledge Sharing only works among active partners. A living stone would not stand back and let the others do the work. A living stone moves, has ideas of his and her own and will not simply accept being put in a specific place. Living stones are experts in their own right. Being a living stone implies that professionalism and experience count, and are valued. Living stones are not subject to the external will of an architect or facilitator but take part and do unexpected things, thereby making their contributions even more valuable.

This part is especially important for those who consider themselves to be in the role of supporters or donors: there is no stepping back to an observant or supporting role. Whoever wants to support in Knowledge Sharing must learn as well. There is no such thing as 'your process' that I support, only 'our process.' This is a hard pill to swallow for those who have always tended to see themselves as outside the game.

Methods competence

Finally, methods competence refers to the ability to create room for Knowledge Sharing and its outcome, co-creation, by jointly finding new answers to unasked questions. This includes the ability to shape contexts to ensure that they are conducive to Knowledge Sharing. Methods competence therefore has several dimensions. First it refers to the capacity to facilitate Knowledge Sharing and ensure that the intended goals are reached. Secondly, it refers to the provision of conditions in organisations and societies that favor Knowledge Sharing.

The facilitation of Knowledge Sharing is mainly a matter of building trust among participants, encouraging contributions and giving a voice to stakeholders that feel less confident to articulate their opinions and experiences, be it because they come from a disadvantaged position or because they have

---

62   Freire 1973: 38, taken from an unpublished quote by José Luiz Fiori.

less practice speaking freely in public. Hence what has been said above about personal competence and social competence proves to be essential for the facilitation of Knowledge Sharing. The ability to step back from a leading role, to respect differences and personal openness to learning are key requisites for Knowledge Sharing. There is a mutual benefit between Knowledge Sharing and empowerment.

Apart from these soft skills, facilitation of Knowledge Sharing also requires abilities in results oriented management: formulating clear goals, monitoring progress and evaluating whether the expected impacts have been achieved, leadership capacities, teamwork etc.[63]. Project management is not limited to the ability to use certain tools, but also the capacity to question and adapt them to the context. This also requires a basic understanding of the reform processes towards which shared knowledge is expected to contribute and the political conditions under which these are likely to prosper.

It is important to stress that facilitation of Knowledge Sharing as horizontal cooperation is not necessarily, or at least not exclusively, the task of a facilitator who guides the group, but rather a shared responsibility of all group members. Regarding the possible design of reform projects as an outcome of Knowledge Sharing[64], naturally all participants must know their own system and society where reforms are to be implemented. Nevertheless, when it comes to co-creation, the combination of different knowledge elements into new answers and strategies, all participants need a basic understanding of how reforms work and how implementation is enhanced. Knowledge Sharing that results in unrealistic ideas of what is achievable easily ends in frustration when participants back home face day-to-day obstacles to change.

Organisations are not necessarily Knowledge Sharing friendly. There is a potential tension between, on one hand, a hierarchy's need to control a process by which activities are carried out efficiently, and to protect knowledge created within the organisation against third party access, and the open, people-centered approach of Knowledge Sharing on the other. To take part in Knowledge Sharing, organisations therefore need to relinquish intellectual property rights, at least partially, and give a certain freedom to staff members participating in Knowledge Sharing to argue freely, present

---

63   On project and cooperation management, see for instance GIZ 2015.
64   See for instance the case of the Alliance for Financial Inclusion (AFI).

and develop own thoughts in order to create the "challenging linkage between line management and networks"[65]. Accordingly, an organisation's knowledge management, staff development and innovation policies are the most important starting point for creating favorable conditions for Knowledge Sharing. Another important aspect is organisational culture.

In societies, openness towards external influences and the recognition of outsiders' capabilities is key. A clear national identity, freedom of opinion and for private sector and civil society organisations, respect for minorities and norms of non-discrimination are helpful factors for Knowledge Sharing. This does not mean that Knowledge Sharing with members of less free societies would be impossible, but conditions in which participants are working, cultural differences and forms of expression must be kept in mind to make Knowledge Sharing successful. It should also be acknowledged that fears regarding processes being too open are common in western societies that consider themselves free. Data-protection issues also have reasons for existing and should not be overruled thoughtlessly. Finally, the issue of "free-riding" is a problem sometimes, when knowledge is shared freely without proper rules for sustaining knowledge as a commons[66].

What is built through Knowledge Sharing is ideally a new set of ideas, answers and solutions, but also better relations between participating organisations[67]. Together these effects shape what is called "the spiritual house" in the opening quote to this article. As mentioned above, Knowledge Sharing is especially apt where problems and methods for their solution are still to be defined and needs for innovation are greatest. Thus, Knowledge Sharing must make room for a creative process where errors are allowed and out-of-the-box thinking is encouraged. There is no guarantee that innovation will emerge, but the potential for this is highest when ideas flow freely and there is little pressure to come up with pre-defined results before the sharing process has even started.

---

65   Schwaab/Seibold 2014: 163.
66   For appropriate rules and incentives for sharing, see Seibold 2014.
67   See Box 3.

Box 3: Mutual Institutional Strengthening by National Auditing Authorities of Chile and Peru

The National Auditing Authorities of both Chile and Peru have recently developed innovative systems for the control of public works, with the perspective of increased territorial outreach of citizen inclusion through the use of modern information technologies. As part of a project implemented through the Latin American-German Triangular Cooperation Fund from April 2014 to December 2015, both authorities exchanged information on their respective programs, organized study tours and trainings, introduced innovation based on lessons learnt from the dialogue and improved their overall relationship to one another. In this way they were able to benefit from the comparative advantages of their partners' programs –particularly Chile's geographic approach and Peru's client-oriented strategies. At the same time, both authorities and their programs gained international visibility and increased their leadership. Germany contributed with process facilitation and international technical expertise on the topics discussed. The overall contributions to the project totaled approximately 700,000 Euros, which were provided in equal shares by the three countries, partially in cash and partially in kind (workdays of experts and materials).

The project evaluation identified the following success factors[68]:

1. At the beginning of the project, partners' needs and expectations were identified and incorporated into a joint implementation plan;
2. In order to reduce the absence of experts from their workplaces, part of the Knowledge Sharing was done using virtual formats and videoconferences;
3. The mutual strengthening of the two authorities incentivized the intensity of their commitment because they saw they were able to benefit from the cooperation and give highly valued contributions of their own;
4. High level political will and commitment allowed quicker decision making;
5. Once the relationship was established, the appreciation of the project was so high on both sides that it was not affected by political changes.

---

68   Fondo Regional para la Cooperación Triangular en América Latina y el Caribe 2016.

Conclusion: Why Knowledge Sharing is so important today

The analysis of past lessons learned in international development cooperation and of particular cases of Knowledge Sharing, here briefly presented in text-boxes, underline that Knowledge Sharing has significant potential for achieving development goals using a strongly partnership-oriented approach. Nonetheless, Knowledge Sharing is a demanding task that requires a mix of personal competences in the partners involved, as well as openness and political will at an institutional and societal level.

In order to make Knowledge Sharing work, several steps must be taken that imply a serious investment of resources by those who wish to engage in Knowledge Sharing. Some of the most important of these steps towards Knowledge Sharing, as pointed out in this article, are:

- form an attitude of openness towards diversity and co-creation,
- connect self-reflection with a deepening understanding of and interaction with the other,
- link professionalism with the ability to stand back and loosen control,
- learn to use key tools and apply them in a context-specific way,
- make improbable encounters happen and use their potential to combine existing knowledge into new answers and solutions.
- create a Knowledge Sharing friendly ambience in organisations and societies, revising incentives as well as rules and regulations.

Applied in such a way, Knowledge Sharing leads to a new quality of cooperation among equals that corresponds with the requirements of today's multi-polar world. Knowledge Sharing is especially useful for facing challenges where goals have not yet been commonly understood and good answers are still being sought. It reflects basic ideas of the Agenda 2030 (universal agenda, new global partnership, means of implementation) and therefore shows promise as a tool for the implementation of the SDGs. With its strong commitment to respecting difference and otherness, Knowledge Sharing has the potential to counterbalance current trends of polarisation, separation and violence. Knowledge Sharing also fits well with new identities and technical opportunities in the digital world.

Bibliography

Acemoglu, Daron/Robinson, James (2012): Why Nations Fail. The Origins of Power. Prosperity and Poverty, Profile Books, London.

Ambadar, David (2016): Alliance for Financial Inclusion. Bringing smart policies to life, GIZ internal presentation, Eschborn.

Ayala Martínez, Citlali/Müller, Ulrich (2014): Implementation, Ownership, Cooperation as Challenges of Global Governance, in: Lázaro Rüther, Lena/Ayala Martínez, Citlali/Müller, Ulrich (eds.): Global Funds and Networks. Narrowing the Gap between Global Policies and National Implementation, Nomos, Baden-Baden, pp. 27-62.

Chambers, Robert (1994): Foreword, in: Scoones, Ian/ Thompson John (eds.): Beyond farmer first. Rural people's knowledge, agricultural research and extension practice, Exeter, pp. xiii-xvi.

Fondo Regional para la Cooperación Triangular en América Latina y el Caribe (2016): Proyecto "Fortalecimiento interinstitucional para los sistemas territoriales de control de obras para fomentar la transparencia y la participación", Informe final para un proyecto financiado por el Fondo, Deutsche Gesellschaft für Internationale Zusammenarbeit, GIZ (internal document), Lima, Santiago de Chile.

Frank, Andre Gunder (1969): The development of underdevelopment, in: Frank, Andre Gunder: Latin America. Underdevelopment or revolution. Essays on the Development of Underdevelopment and the Immediate Enemy, Monthly Review Press, New York and London, pp. 3-17.

Freire Paulo (1973): Pädagogik der Unterdrückten. Bildung als Praxis der Freiheit, Rowohlt, Reinbek bei Hamburg.

Friedmann, John (1992): Empowerment. The Politics of Alternative Development, Blackwell, Cambridge, Massachusetts and Oxford, UK.

Fukuyama, Francis (2011): The Origins of Political Order, Farrar, Straus and Giroux, New York.

GIZ (Deutsche Gesellschaft für Internationale Zusammenarbeit) (2015): Cooperation Management for Practitioners - Managing Social Change with Capacity WORKS, Springer Gabler, Wiesbaden.

Hannig, Alfred/Lee, Sung-Ah/Leifheit, Maren/Lázaro, Lena (2015): The AFI Approach. A new model for International Cooperation. Alliance for Financial Inclusion (AFI), Deutsche Gesellschaft für Internationale Zusammenarbeit (GIZ), Bill and Melinda Gates Foundation, Eschborn.

Hannig, Alfred/Leifheit, Maren/ Lázaro-Rüther, Lena (2014): The Alliance for Financial Inclusion: Bringing Smart Policies to Life, in: Lázaro Rüther, Lena/Ayala Martínez, Citlali/Müller, Ulrich (eds.): Global Funds and Networks. Narrowing the Gap between Global Policies and National Implementation, Nomos, Baden-Baden, pp. 199-208.

Jann, Werner (2009): Dimensions of Political Steering. Definitions, Questions, Conditions, Practice, GTZ Conference: How to Manage the Unmanageable? Supporting Political Steering for Development Results, Berlin.

Johnstone, Keith (1981): Impro. Improvisation and the Theatre, Methuen Publishing, UK.

Krewer, Bernd/ Uhlmann, Adelheid (2015): Models for Human Capacity Development. Didactics Concept of the Academy for International Cooperation, Deutsche Gesellschaft für Internationale Zusammenarbeit (GIZ), Bonn.

Lasuén, José Ramón (1973): Urbanisation and Development - the Temporal Interaction between Geographical and Sectoral Clusters, in: Urban Studies, Vol. 10(2), pp. 163-188.

Laws, Edward/Leftwich, Adrian (2012): Bringing History Back In: Three Big Books. Summaries and some questions, Background Paper 09, Developmental Leadership Program.

Leutner, Jana/Müller, Ulrich (2010): Ownership in Practice, in: Frenken, Sarah/Müller, Ulrich (eds.): Ownership and Political Steering in Developing Countries, Nomos, Baden-Baden, pp. 47-59.

Leutner, Jana/Rösch, Michael (2014): Global Networks. Extractive Industries Transparency Initiative, in: Lázaro Rüther, Lena/Ayala Martínez, Citlali/Müller, Ulrich (eds.): Global Funds and Networks. Narrowing the Gap between Global Policies and National Implementation, Nomos, Baden-Baden, pp. 209-220.

Meadows, Graham (2014): Beyond "Us" and "Them", in: Lázaro Rüther, Lena/Ayala Martínez, Citlali/Müller, Ulrich (eds.): Global Funds and Networks. Narrowing the Gap between Global Policies and National Implementation, Nomos, Baden-Baden, pp. 297-299.

Müller, Ulrich/Knodt Michèle (2012): Human Resources in Triangular Cooperation, in: Langendorf, Julia/Piefer, Nadine/Knodt, Michèle/Müller, Ulrich/Lázaro Rüther, Lena (eds.): Triangular Cooperation. A guideline for working in practice, Nomos, Baden-Baden, pp. 141-158.

Müller, Ulrich/Kenngott, Carola (2009): Mehr als die Vermittlung von Fachwissen. Aktuelle Herausforderungen, Trends und Ansätze der Beratung in der Entwicklungszusammenarbeit, Geographie und Schule, Vol. 181, pp. 24-31.

Müller, Ulrich (ed.) (1999): Planificando el Uso de la Tierra. Catálogo de herramientas y experiencias, GTZ, Eschborn.

Mummert, Annette/Mummert, Uwe (2010): Success Factors for Strategic Development Management, in: Frenken, Sarah/Müller, Ulrich (eds.): Ownership and Political Steering in Developing Countries. Proceedings of international conferences in London and Berlin, Nomos, Baden-Baden, pp. 31-46.

North, Douglass C./Wallis, John Joseph/Weingast, Barry R. (2009): Violence and Social Orders. A Conceptual Framework for Interpreting Recorded Human History, Cambridge University Press, Cambridge.

Raymond, Eric Steven (2000): The Cathedral and the Bazaar. Accessible under: http.//www.catb.org/~esr/writings/cathedral-bazaar/cathedral-bazaar/ (02.07.2016).

Salas, Maria Angélica (1994): 'The technicians only believe in science and cannot read the sky'. The cultural dimension of the knowledge conflict in the Andes, in: Scoones, Ian/Thompson, John (eds.): Beyond farmer first. Rural people's knowledge, agricultural research and extension practice, Exeter, pp. 57-69.

Schätzl, Ludwig (1986): Wirtschaftsgeographie 3 Politik, Schöningh, Paderborn.

Schwaab, Jan/Seibold, Balthas (2014): The potential of networks for strengthening the sustainability of development cooperation, in: Lázaro Rüther, Lena/Ayala Martínez, Citlali/Müller, Ulrich (eds.): Global Funds and Networks. Narrowing the Gap between Global Policies and National Implementation, Nomos, Baden-Baden, pp. 157-178.

Seibold, Balthas (2014): Learning by Sharing. How global communities cultivate skills and capacity through peer-production of knowledge, in: GIZ (Deutsche Gesellschaft für Internationale Zusammenarbeit) (ed.): 10 trends in open innovation. How to leverage social media for new forms of cooperation, GIZ.

Thompson, Wilbur (1965): A preface to Urban Economics, John Hopkins Press, Baltimore.

Thrupp, Lori Ann/Cabarle, Bruce/Zazueta, Aaron (1994): Participatory methods and political processes. Linking grassroot actions to policy-making for sustainable development in Latin America, in: Scoones, Ian/ Thompson John (eds.): Beyond farmer first. Rural people's knowledge, agricultural research and extension practice, Exeter, pp. 170-177.

United Nations (2015): Sustainable Development Goals. Accessible under: http://www.un.org/sustainabledevelopment/sustainable-development-goals/ (10.20.2017).

Ziemer, Gesa (2015): Kollektives Arbeiten, in: Haarmann, Anke/Rey, Anton/Schenker, Christoph/Mersch, Dieter/Pérez, Germán Toro/Badura, Jens/Dubach, Selma (eds.): Künstlerische Forschung. Ein Handbuch, diaphanes, Zürich, pp. 169-172.

Personal Learning, Organisational Change and Social Consensus – Added Value Dimensions of Knowledge Sharing in Latin America

Iris Dagmar Barth, Ulrich Müller and Anna Julia Fiedler

Introduction

When in the early 1990s the economist Peter F. Drucker announced "the shift to the knowledge society", there seemed to be little doubt about the added value of knowledge related activities, because in the "post capitalist society [...] the basic economic resource [...] is and will be knowledge"[1]. Nevertheless, the term knowledge society remained controversial, as did the ways knowledge was dealt with.

Peter Drucker saw "the forces that are creating post-capitalist society" as originating in what he called "the developed world": only there, he concluded, could "the challenges, the opportunities, the problems of post-capitalist society" be adequately handled[2]. This bipolar concept of the world has been greatly eroded over the last two decades. Subsequently, doubts have also arisen regarding the dynamics of knowledge transfer from the "developed world", where it was assumed to be created, to "developing countries", where it was assumed to be needed.

This shift in perspectives on global relations is expressed in the 2030 Agenda for Sustainable Development that postulates the joint responsibility of all peoples and all countries for "a comprehensive, far-reaching and people-centred set of universal and transformative goals and targets"[3]. It is an Agenda in which the dimensions of sustainability are connected, different stakeholders interact and no one is left behind. Latin American countries in particular have supported this egalitarian aspect in the negotiation of the Agenda.

Regarding approaches to dealing with knowledge, this means converting the traditional North-South transfer of techniques and knowledge into a co-

---

1   Drucker 1993: 5-7.
2   Ibid.: 13.
3   United Nations 2015: 3.

constructed process of knowledge that equally involves partners from all parts of the world: Knowledge Sharing. The Global Partnership on Knowledge Sharing initiated by the World Bank in 2016 is therefore convinced that Knowledge Sharing will be critical to the achievement of the Sustainable Development Goals, as stressed by global development agreements such as the Addis Ababa Action Agenda and the Agenda 2030[4].

This process of co-construction is closely related to a team's capacity to capitalize on a diversity of perspectives. Multiple cooperation partners may share similar experiences, but nonetheless hold differing perspectives. It is much more likely that new solutions and innovations will be found among several partners with different points of view and different approaches to problem solving. Diversity and the openness to accept such diversity are very important factors for success, and are also crucial values of Knowledge Sharing. Plurality in perspectives from different partners allows for a better understanding of where the energies and obstacles are in the existing system[5].

Nevertheless, understood thus, Knowledge Sharing is a demanding process and requires of the partners involved capacities that cannot simply be assumed[6]. Therefore, in order to create the necessary conditions for Knowledge Sharing, an investment must be made that can be justified in relation to the expected outcome. Here the added value comes in: the positive results that can be expected from Knowledge Sharing to support the required effort.

Based on these ideas, this chapter will further explore the added value of Knowledge Sharing. It is a side product of a study initiated by the World Bank, OECD (Organisation for Economic Co-operation and Development) and GIZ on monitoring and evaluating Knowledge Sharing in the context of the Global Partnership on Country-led Knowledge Sharing (GPKS). It builds on the approaches of German Development Cooperation to learning and cooperation management. Following two sections focusing on the definition of Knowledge Sharing and the variety of Knowledge Sharing experiences in Latin America, these approaches will be briefly introduced. Then, the chapter's central focus will be to develop and summarise the added value dimensions of Knowledge Sharing. Finally, some reflections on the measurement of these added values will be presented.

---

4   GPKS 2016: 1.
5   Piefer et al. 2015: 10.
6   See the chapter by Ulrich Müller in this book.

Knowledge Sharing: practical challenges and blurred terminology

If knowledge, as Peter Drucker argued in the 1990s, is a key strategic denominator in the societies of today, all subsequent argumentation must start with the definition of knowledge. According to John Erpenbeck and Werner Sauter[7], knowledge in a narrow sense comprises the combination of data and information, knowledge on methods, general expertise, knowing and core elements of logic.

Knowledge is subjectively represented and reconstructed in different ways and expressions by the individual. Subjective knowledge emerges, as Alfred Schütz and Thomas Luckmann[8] put it, from the sedimented subjective experiences in the lifeworld. Based on subjective knowledge a "social stock of knowledge" is formed through intersubjective processes of objectification, shaping of social relevance and institutionalized procedures of knowledge transfer. The social stock of knowledge flows back into the establishment of subjective knowledge[9] because each individual is socially embedded.

This dialectic of subjective and social knowledge establishes a permanent process of Knowledge Sharing under conditions in which a totally equal social distribution of knowledge is impossible[10]. The more complex and differentiated the emerging fields of specialized knowledge, the more complex the social distribution of knowledge and the power relations between experts and amateurs, and the more demanding the task of Knowledge Sharing. What is needed is far "more than mere communication"[11]. Andreea Serban and Jing Luan[12] therefore consider Knowledge Sharing as far more important than the technology that provides simple and efficient ways of information transfer. Nevertheless, preparing individuals to share what they know "is one of the toughest nuts" to be cracked[13].

---

7   Erpenbeck/Sauter 2013: 28-29.
8   Schütz/Luckmann 1994: 363.
9   Ibid.: 379.
10   Ibid.: 366.
11   Janus 2016: 4.
12   Serban/Luan 2002: 12.
13   Bukowitz/Williams 1999, cited in: Serban/Luan 2002: 12.

Perhaps because of these difficulties, the way the term Knowledge Sharing is used remains rather blurred.[14] The range of possible definitions extends from not-necessarily-focused exchanges of ideas between individuals and groups on an equal footing to a unidirectional communication between a sender who knows and a recipient who assimilates this knowledge. There are also different views on whether Knowledge Sharing is exclusively bound to individuals or can also take place between groups or organisations. Finally, some doubt has even been expressed as to whether knowledge can be shared at all, since it is always context-bound. Dan Paulin and Kaj Suneson[15] therefore distinguish "several levels" where "contradictions and discrepancies between the definitions (of Knowledge Sharing) can be found:

- Sharing taking place between individuals only versus between individuals, teams, units or organisations
- Focused or unfocused versus clearly focused
- A transaction versus saying that knowledge can never be shared
- Unidirectional versus multidirectional"

Based on these distinctions, this chapter takes a definition of Knowledge Sharing as the focused, multidirectional transaction between individuals, groups of individuals, organisations and societies.

This choice is made for several reasons. Although it might be philosophically interesting to consider the question of whether knowledge can be shared at all, as far as collaboration is concerned, transaction – as truncated as it may be – matters. From the same point of view, it is the focused transaction that matters and not so much the accidental or unfocused one. Nevertheless, demanding that Knowledge Sharing should be "clearly focused" might be neither realistic nor sufficiently consider the value of "sidesteps," which are extremely important where transfer of tacit knowledge is concerned. The preference towards multidirectional sharing is bound to the basic ideas of the Agenda 2030. It also acknowledges the importance of "learning through others"[16]. Finally, the idea that sharing takes place between individuals, organisations and societies is based on the fact that it is

---

14   See Dan Paulin and Kaj Suneson in the title of their 2012 article: "Knowledge Transfer, Knowledge Sharing and Knowledge Barriers – Three Blurry Terms in KM;" the following arguments are taken from their text.
15   Paulin/Suneson 2012: 83.
16   Krewer/Uhlmann 2015: 17.

not possible to reduce interaction and social categories to the attributes of individuals.[17]

Knowledge Sharing activities vary along a broad spectrum, ranging from relatively closed groups characterized by mutual trust to the co-production of open knowledge. Concrete activities related to that scope may be one-off events, accompanied processes, virtual or face-to-face communities or collaborative production – among others. Successful Knowledge Sharing can be achieved through[18]:

- Sharing conferences where stakeholders meet over several sessions, exchanging ideas, building networks and finding inspiration.
- BarCamps at which groups of peers organize open learning and innovation processes for themselves, where everyone is allowed to join in and speak.
- Study trips on which a selected group of actors meets their peers in other contexts, with the objective of generating innovation.
- Labs in which different actors meet with the idea of creating an impact on local and regional issues, setting international agendas or sharing knowledge with social movements.
- Sharing networks where virtual and face-to-face communities of practitioners exchange and co-create.
- Open source solution platforms where collaborative production of open knowledge is generated.

In international cooperation, Knowledge Sharing is currently used within many different constellations of actors such as networks, triangular cooperation, multi-stakeholder partnerships, but also for more traditional bi- and multilateral projects and programs. This happens on single occasions or within series of events that are related to one another.

---

17   Although Anthony Giddens (1995: 277-278) argues that only individuals, beings with bodily existence, can be actors, the consequences of actions go beyond the sum of individual intentions, decisions and finally actions themselves. Actions relate to each other and the results of former actions influence and limit the options individuals have (Werlen 1995: 42). The sequence of mutual influences is endless. Therefore, it cannot be said that agency determines structure nor vice versa (Giddens 1995: 277).

18   GIZ 2015.

Figure 1: Where does knowledge Sharing take place

		Formats		
		Face to face	Virtual	Joint action
Dimensions	Single occasions			
	Networks			
	Projects			
	Within organisations and societies			
	Between organisations and societies			

Source: Draft by the authors

Knowledge Sharing in Latin America: A variety of experiences

The range of practical experiences of Knowledge Sharing in Latin America is as wide as the possible definitions and applications of Knowledge Sharing itself. Several contributions to this volume go some way toward reflecting this tendency.

Knowledge Sharing takes place where extension agents start taking farmers' experiences seriously and develop new solutions together with them, as Horacio Rodriguez points out in his chapter, where indigenous knowledge is recognized and incorporated into the improvement of land-use practices.

Knowledge Sharing also happens within and between organisations that exchange their experiences in similar tasks, and by doing so enrich their processes and standards. This is the case with collaboration occurring between the National Auditing Authorities of Chile and Peru, presented in Box 3 of the chapter by Ulrich Müller[19]. In this context, it is worth mentioning that Latin America is rich in cross country networks of organisations such as specializing in many topics such as metrology,[20] as well as central

---

19   See the chapter by Ulrich Müller in this book, pp. 13-20.
20   Inter-american Metrology System (SIM).

auditing authorities,[21] public prosecutor's offices,[22] ombudsperson offices,[23] tax administrations[24] etc. These networks generally engage in Knowledge Sharing on a technical level, often addressing quite down-to-earth, operational questions from a country-to-country perspective. In the field of metrology, for instance, in the late 2000s the responsible institutes in several Latin American countries established a peer reviewing mechanism for mutual quality control. While on these technical visits, experts from other countries analysed the compliance of the reviewed institute with internationally established standards and gave concrete recommendations for improvement. Since the visits were mutual, they helped to increase self-esteem of technical staff and trust between the institutes.[25] In these sharing processes, the fact that most countries in Latin America share Spanish as a common language – and that Portuguese is sufficiently close to make communication easy – is an important factor for success. This is additionally enhanced by rather similar historical experiences and related legal systems due to a shared colonial and post-colonial history.

In a number of cases, the Latin American perspective also exerts an important influence over global networks on the topic. An example of this is the Latin American Network of Rural Extension Services (RELASER).[26] It was created in 2010 in Chile under the umbrella of the Global Forum for Rural Advisory Services, a network that is working with private and public extension services around the world. RELASER supports the consolidation of public and private extension services in Latin America and the exchange of experiences on different aspects of their work. One of the pillars of RELASER is the creation and management of spaces for dialogue and Knowledge Sharing (virtual and face-to-face) to generate, evolve and improve capacities and results between individuals and organisations (public and private). Topics for Knowledge Sharing in RELASER are the development of curricula for extension services, the modernisation and improvement of policy makers' capacities, a 'new' profile for extension workers and the development of different instruments and methods to provide evidence of the results and impacts of the extension services. The network not

---

21   Organisation of Latin American and Caribbean Supreme Audit Institutions (OLACEFS).
22   Ibero American Association of Public Prosecutors (AIAMP).
23   Ibero-American Federation of Ombudsman (FIO).
24   International Centre for Tropical Agriculture (CIAT).
25   Interview by Ulrich Müller on September 21, 2010 with staff of the National Institute of Technology, Normalisation and Metrology (INTN) in Paraguay.
26   For further information see: http://www.relaser.org (10.28.2017).

only pushes the exchange of knowledge on an international level, but also strengthens dialogue within its member countries between farmers, public and private extension services and academic actors. RELASER also aims at Knowledge Sharing with other networks focused on related subjects, such as family farming, innovation and research. The instruments used by RELASER for Knowledge Sharing vary from national fora, working groups and workshops to meetings and virtual platforms. RELASER is organized by a steering committee, an executive secretariat and members who may be individuals or institutions.

Latin American countries also directly engage in strong and effective participation in global Knowledge Sharing networks. A good example is the Alliance for Financial Inclusion (AFI) that brings together "high-ranking officials from central banks, finance ministries and other regulatory bodies" in a peer learning approach[27]. In four years, AFI has developed "more than 50 policy changes in member countries" and become "an implementing partner of the G-20 Global Partnership for Financial Inclusion (GPFI) and the G-20 Financial Inclusion Peer Learning Program"[28]. The Global Policy Forum 2011 in Mexico led to the endorsement of the "Maya Declaration on Financial Inclusion … the world's first set of measurable commitments to increase access to formal financial services for the world's 2.5 billion un-banked"[29]. In the Americas 25 organisations from 18 countries are members of AFI.[30] A very different kind of global network is the Extractive Industries Transparency Initiative, EITI. In contrast to AFI, EITI is a multi-stake-holder platform where governments, companies, investors and civil society organisations come together with the aim of enhancing "transparency of payments in the extractive sector", fostering "public debate" and thus im-proving "the governance of public revenues from the extractive sector"[31]. Among the EITI members in Latin America up to March 2017, Peru has achieved "meaningful progress" in meeting the 2016 EITI standard, while Colombia, the Dominican Republic, Guatemala and Honduras are yet to be assessed against the standard.[32]

---

27   Hannig et al. 2014: 202. On this case see also Box 2 of Ulrich Müller's chapter in this volume.
28   Hannig et al. 2014: 205.
29   Ibid.: 205.
30   For the current list of members see: http://www.afi-global.org/members/ (03.21.2017).
31   Leutner/Rösch 2014: 209.
32   For further information see: https://eiti.org/countries (03.17.2017).

Apart from such networks, Latin American countries also make use of Knowledge Sharing on specific occasions with the intention of bringing forward a particular national goal. An example can be found in the efforts of the Mexican Agency for International Development Cooperation, (AMEXCID), to establish a National Register of International Development Cooperation. Transparency in International Development Cooperation is one of the key issues in the debate on effective development cooperation strongly promoted by the International Aid Transparency Initiative (IATI), which aims to make "information about aid spending easier to access, use, and understand."[33] The quantification of development cooperation activities poses a challenge to coordination bodies in that field, since many actors from different sectors and levels of government, civil society and the private sector take part in the development cooperation activities of a country. Reporting on these activities requires standards for data provision that reflect the particular requirements of many different forms of cooperation, and which can easily be understood by all parties expected to report. In the OECD Development Assistance Committee's member countries, these requirements have resulted in the elaboration of complex guidelines[34]. In emerging countries, the establishment of the corresponding norms and regulations is connected with the development of the institutional set-up for development cooperation. In Mexico, the Law of International Development Cooperation (LCID) of 2011[35] "provided the legal basis and a comprehensive framework to strengthen a system of cooperation, formalize practices and leverage the role of Mexico as development partner"[36]. Apart from the creation of the Mexican Cooperation Agency, AMEXCID, in 2011, one of the instruments provided for by the law is the Registry and Information System of International Development Cooperation[37]. This has been considered by AMEXCID as a "coordination and process design challenge because of the particular characteristics of South-South cooperation: the diversity of actors involved … and the fragmentation of information about the projects"[38]. Therefore, in order to establish the necessary stand-

---

33   For further information see: http://www.aidtransparency.net/about
       (02.02.2017).
34   OECD 2016.
35   Gobierno de México 2011.
36   Vega 2014: 83.
37   Ibid.: 86.
38   Borbolla 2014: 63-64.

ards for this registry, AMEXCID adopted a Knowledge Sharing approach. In 2012 a Catalogue of Mexican Capacities was elaborated with the cooperation of the Japanese Cooperation Agency (JICA), as a kind of stocktaking of Mexican Cooperation experiences[39]. In 2013, a workshop on international experiences in the quantification of cooperation activities was held in Mexico City in coordination with the German International Development Cooperation Agency (GIZ), and enabled an exchange of experiences regarding the necessary regulations with participants from Brazil, Chile, EU, Germany, OECD DAC, Spain and Turkey. A comparison of the cases presented by participants set a solid basis for AMEXCID to define their needs and set-up a realistic and manageable framework within the National Registry of International Development Cooperation (RENCID) that provides yearly data on Mexican Development Cooperation. Transparency in Mexican Cooperation activities is documented in a study on the perception of Mexican International Development Cooperation, although there is also a demand for incorporating additional actors into reporting[40], which could be achieved by gradually extending the scope of RENCID.

Finally, Knowledge Sharing in Latin America is also an issue concerning whole societies. An illustrative example of this is the chapter on the Bolivian Constitutional Reform from 2009, presented by Iván Égido in this volume.

Approaches to conceptualizing the added value of Knowledge Sharing

In order to gain a more systematic view on the benefits of Knowledge Sharing, this article builds on two approaches developed by GIZ in the fields of competence and capacity development. Both approaches have been derived from practice and are meant to be applied in practice. They adopt experiences of successful cooperation projects and are embedded in practice-oriented guidelines and toolkits, namely the didactic concept of GIZ's Academy for International Cooperation (AIZ)[41] and GIZ's management model Capacity WORKS[42].

---

39   AMEXCID/JICA 2012.
40   Pérez et al. 2015: 140.
41   Krewer/Uhlmann 2015.
42   GIZ 2015.

The first approach[43] broadens the understanding of the content of Knowledge Sharing by distinguishing the dimensions of knowledge, ability and attitude. Knowledge, ability and attitude form central components of human capacity to act in open, complex, dynamic and sometimes chaotic situations in a creative and self-organized way[44]. Here, knowledge is the subjective cognitive representation of information and data about the world that is formalized and objectified in different ways. Ability refers to the capacity to apply forms of action that are appropriate to the respective situation. This is achieved through automated capabilities in stereotyped areas of demand that are acquired through practice[45]. Finally, attitude in psychology is a general and situation-specific disposition to act. As a value-based motivation and identification, it plays a substantial role in activating a concrete action. "Attitude is a psychological construct. It is a mental and emotional entity that inheres in, or characterizes, the person."[46]. The concept of attitude is also increasingly used in approaches of political science and pedagogy concerned with individual resilience as a general competence in unpredictable and frequently changing contexts[47]. It is important to note that attitude is not fixed, but rather evolves based on constant reflection and self-questioning[48]. There is a permanent interplay between the development of competencies within the dimensions of knowledge, ability and attitude, which forms the backbone of the development of personality.

Knowledge, ability and attitude reflect the different didactic priorities in capacity building required for a broadened goal of learning that links cognitive development, practice oriented skills and a holistic understanding of personality[49]. This is based on the experience in development cooperation practice that the mere acquisition or transfer of knowledge does not guarantee change per se. Development happens when personal, social, technical and methodological competences meet – thinking, feeling and acting, or head (knowledge), hands (ability) and heart (attitude).

Knowledge Sharing is a joint learning process in which learning is a co-construction between learners and "teachers" or "trainers." It is a complex action with different stages of maturation at the personal, organisational or

---

43   Many thanks to Bernd Krewer for his guidance on the conceptualisation of knowledge, ability and attitude for the purposes of this article.

44   Erpenbeck/Rosenstichl 2007: XVII ff.

45   Erpenbeck/Sauter 2013: 32.

46   Perloff 2016: 38.

47   Kath 2016; Jonas et al. 2014.

48   Krewer/Uhlmann, 2015: 13.

49   Arnold 2012; Arnold 2010; Sauter/Staudt 2016; Sauter/Scholz 2015.

societal level, which may be understood as a progression of cognitive, motivational and affective elements. In this sense knowledge, ability and attitude are the main pillars for a professional understanding of Knowledge Sharing and learning processes. The capacity for action in a systemic understanding is always an interaction between individual, organisational and social dispositions. To really reach sustainable changes, organisations and societies need strong, active and self-responsible people who are able to contribute their personal experience, knowledge, abilities and creativity to complex processes of change[50].

This leads directly to the second approach to be used here: the distinctions of person, organisation and society as different and complementary levels of intervention in development cooperation contexts. The distinction between the levels person, organisation and society stands at the center of the capacity development strategy in GIZ's management model Capacity WORKS[51]. Capacity development is a holistic process. Capacity in this context means the ability of persons, organisations and societies to shape their own development in a sustainable way and to adapt to dynamic contexts. It would be unrealistic to suppose that a single person, because of newly acquired knowledge, skills and attitude, could single-handedly change an organisation or even a society. On the other hand, practical experience also shows many top-down organisational and social changes that failed because they did not sufficiently consider the interests, capabilities and also obstructive potential of persons within these organisations and societies.

Nevertheless, learning is often unilaterally associated with persons. Less is known about the learning of organisations and societies, because such processes appear more complex and abstract. Organisations and societies are more than the sum of their members. They build structures, processes, rules and rituals that are adapted when changing situations make it necessary[52]. Therefore, it can be said that organisations and societies learn by adapting their structures, processes, rules and rituals. Organisations and societies do not only learn when their members learn, but also when they reform their procedures and settings.

Societies and organisations form a social stock of knowledge that is constantly developing due to a constant influx of new experiences, while other

---

50   Krewer/Uhlmann, 2015: 7.
51   GIZ 2015: 124-130.
52   GIZ 2015: 87.

elements of the social stock of knowledge are questioned when they prove insufficient to cope with a specific situation[53]. There is a complex interaction between subjective individual knowledge and the social stock of knowledge. In order to deal with these processes and to make sure that elements of knowledge are kept and transferred from generation to generation[54], societies and organisations establish processes and structures to store knowledge in libraries, transmit it through educational processes and reconstruct it by matching different points of view and experiences. Organisations establish knowledge management units and create databases containing the organisation's knowledge, which are often heavily protected. They even develop a language of their own that cannot easily be understood by outsiders that have not been socialized into the organisation. In the same way, societies create complex education and mass media systems and establish mechanisms for the co-creation of new knowledge by bringing together rather unexpected and unlike partners.

Furthermore, organisations and societies develop abilities through their sets of processes and rules. These enable the maintenance and replication of organisations and societies, and provide them with systematic reactions in moments of crisis. They define how members of organisations and societies can effectively and efficiently meet and interact, bringing them together regardless of the different roles they play.

Finally, the attitudes of organisations and societies can be found in the values, convictions and cultural rituals they develop. The vision and mission statements of organisations, as well as the value systems of societies, determine which processes and rules are developed and how knowledge is dealt with at an organisational and societal level. The individual attitude is strongly influenced by social values but at the same time, these values and the associated rituals are constantly changing. The stability and resilience of societies and organisations depend heavily on their ability to find consensus and organically adapt values and rituals.

The successful management of Knowledge Sharing processes strongly depends on the strengthening of competences at the three levels of intervention:

- Individuals increase their competences and shape learning processes in such a way that they contribute to sustainable changes in their organisations and societies.

---

53   Schütz/Luckmann 1994: 193.
54   Schütz/Luckmann 194: 352ff.

- Organisations improve their processes, rules, standards, visions and missions in order to better achieve their goals, providing individual members with better conditions for carrying out their roles, leading to a greater impact on a societal level.
- Societies improve cooperative and collaborative relationships between their members (individuals and organisations) and adapt general conditions to new challenges.

Together, all three levels procure that Knowledge Sharing based innovations are brought forward and jointly agreed development goals can be achieved more effectively[55].

The Added Value Dimensions of Knowledge Sharing

In this study the added value of Knowledge Sharing is seen as the variety of positive effects on development, generated through Knowledge Sharing activities and processes. These intended or unintended supplementary goals increase the development benefit of activities in which Knowledge Sharing is used as part of development projects or programs. The Agenda 2030[56] names Knowledge Sharing as one of the means of implementation for the Sustainable Development Goals. Hence, the added value of Knowledge Sharing lies in its functionality e.g. towards achieving development goals. However, under what circumstances and in what way is Knowledge Sharing suited to achieving development goals?

An initial answer to this question is that Knowledge Sharing underlines the social dimension of development. Knowledge Sharing is about joint learning and joint responsibility; it is an interactive, complex, mutual and co-constructed process where shared responsibility between different partners is expected to increase the capacity for dealing with differences[57]. Another field in which Knowledge Sharing is expected to yield positive results is the scaling up of development models and solutions which have been successful in one country and might be adapted to others[58]. Finally, there is an expectation that lateral effects, which go beyond immediate contributions to the achievement of development goals, accompany Knowledge

---

55   GIZ 2015: 80.
56   See Sustainable Development Goal 17.6.
57   Krewer/Uhlmann 2015: 3.
58   World Bank 2015b: 19.

Sharing. Knowledge Sharing is attributed with enhancing changes in attitude, culture and practices such as building ownership, trust and consensus. Among the partners involved, such change in itself becomes a resource that improves conditions for the achievement of future goals beyond the case that initially brought the partners together.

In order to gain a more systematic view on the added value of Knowledge Sharing, the concepts presented in part 4 of this article are used to create a matrix that categorizes the added value of Knowledge Sharing according to the categories of knowledge, ability and attitude on the one hand and person, organisation and society on the other[59]. The categories "knowledge, ability and attitude" prove applicable to an analysis of the structural entities "person, organisation and society." Learning by persons, organisations and societies follows distinct rules for each, and means different things. The same is true about the significance of knowledge, ability and attitude on each of these levels. Nevertheless, this does not mean that the different fields in the matrix are totally independent from each other. What happens in one field may restrict progress in another, such as when a person acquires new knowledge, but the organisations and society in which this person is acting do not allow the use of this knowledge. On the other hand, there can be synergies between the various added values, when more knowledge leads to new abilities and changes in attitude, when persons positively influence organisations or when societies improve the overall conditions for persons. These possible effects are multidirectional and there is no single path towards greater improvement. In the same way, the direction of possible obstacles can also be manifold, such as when organisational processes are not ready for improvement, reforms are obstructed by individual persons, or crises at the society level slow the pace of change agents.

---

59   See Figure 2.

Figure 2: Added Value dimensions of Knowledge Sharing

	Knowledge	Ability	Attitude
Person	• Persons have deepened their knowledge.	• Persons have acquired new skills.	• Persons have improved their motivation and self-confidence. • They have reflected more deeply on their personal way of thinking and acting.
Organisation	• Organisations have increased the effectiveness of their knowledge management.	• Organisational processes have improved. • Organisations have become more resilient to external changes.	• Organisations have advanced their visions and standards.
Society	• Social Actors have co-created new solutions to social challenges.	• Connectivity has increased between different stakeholders within societies.	• Consensus within societies has improved.

Source: Created by the authors, based on Krewer/Uhlmann 2015, GIZ 2015 and World Bank 2015a.

The most obvious added value of Knowledge Sharing can be found at the level of individuals. Persons acquire new personal knowledge because they learn from others, which they do more easily when they find that their knowledge is also appreciated and useful to others. Knowledge Sharing on the personal level can lead to a broader awareness or increased understanding of problems, solutions and their interconnections. Subsequently, persons are better informed and count with broader insights to predict the consequences of their actions. Thus, better or new knowledge also helps to develop and enhance personal skills. Individuals change their patterns of planning and evaluating actions and incorporate them into their personal and work related routines. They start to understand that many processes of change are not simply linear, and that they therefore require skills for tackling several different tasks in parallel. They also become aware of the need for greater flexibility and the ability to assess risk. Thus, exchanges between partners from diverse backgrounds with multiple perspectives can be a catalyst for enhanced self-reflection based on shared experiences. This self-reflection encourages changes in attitude. Persons gain greater motivation and self-confidence. This is often encouraged in situations characterized by shared responsibilities, equality and horizontal partnerships, which are closely related to ownership and trust building. Persons, who have the opportunity to learn from and negotiate with others, while adopting a variety of different roles and implementing different choices, will probably emerge more motivated, with greater confidence and courage to generate new processes and innovations.

Persons thus experience that they are able to undergo role changes without compromising the achievement of their goals. They learn to step back and leave the front stage to others, but also to take the lead when necessary, thus increasing their personal repertoire from unilateral dominance or humbleness to the flexibility to act according to what the situation requires. A continuous, habitus reflection is undertaken, which could also lead to more empathy and a better understanding of others' interests. Knowledge Sharing requires the ownership and co-responsibility of all partners involved. Increased personal knowledge, new sets of individual skills and changes in attitude are all enhanced by ownership and co-responsibility. Besides, joint learning from both success and failure, as well as through negotiation between different perspectives and opinions, help to build more empathic relationships among individuals.

While the organisational level shows some similarities with the personal level, it is also different in several ways.

As with individuals, organisations can simply acquire new knowledge throughout Knowledge Sharing processes. However, the range of acquired knowledge in organisations far exceeds that of individuals, calling for changes and improvements to knowledge management. This improvement of knowledge management structures is a common added value at the organisational level. Feedback loops and enhanced analysis methods help to generate more meaningful information, while supporting the establishment of a more efficient and effective working structure within an organisation. Joint learning processes support this kind of management, eventually leading to a higher complementarity of differing perspectives.

Changes in ability represent another added value at the organisational level. In order to be sustainable, improvements in organisational processes must be institutionalized within an organisation through corresponding leadership decisions. On the other hand, organisations must also learn when it is necessary to insist on the application of such institutional rules, and when it is necessary to deal with them more flexibly and improvise when adapting to moments of crisis. This kind of sovereignty in the application of process norms increases organisational resilience, the ability to cope with unplanned, unscheduled and unexpected changes – a very important quality in complex contexts. Furthermore, the horizontal nature of Knowledge Sharing allows for a deeper insight into the tailor-made solutions needed, leading to increased potential for better quality innovation and more creative solutions. Innovation is mostly seen from the technical, product-oriented perspective. But innovation also can be defined as a new way to "achieve goals, especially new forms of organisation, new rules, new lifestyles which change the course of social change and solve problems better than prior practices"[60]. These changes in organisational processes and rules also lead to a revision of organisational visions and standards. Organisations begin to establish procedures that are less hierarchical in nature, declaring "out-of-the-box" thinking to be an essential part of their DNA. They project an image of flexibility and independence for groups assigned to internal projects, as a means to counteract the outdated concept of "bureaucratic dinosaurs".

Knowledge Sharing also can lead to increased willingness to explore new topics and engage in dialogue with potential additional partners in an informal and unofficial way. This creates opportunities for unexpected and often temporary new relationships. Due to the openness of these settings, there is a likelihood of actors coming together in improbable encounters, who would not otherwise have cooperated[61]. In order to describe such creative social settings, which lie beyond the classical social categories of friendship and formal organisations with their hierarchical work relations, the German sociologist Gesa Ziemer[62] developed the concept of "partners in crime": A group of persons joins informally and works together, bringing in different specialties in order to achieve an agreed aim and disbanding after the aim is achieved. While such flexible and creative forms of cooperation may not be surprising in contexts of art production, they are also increasingly also found in economics and development cooperation, as evidenced by the resurgence of interest in networks and informal partnerships. Knowledge

---

60   Zapf 1989: 182, cited in: Piefer et al. 2015: 10.
61   Piefer et al. 2015: 13.
62   Ziemer 2013.

Sharing is an essential element of such forms of cooperation, and one of the key tasks of the temporary group which obtains its strength from the distinctive special characteristics of its members.

On a societal level, Knowledge Sharing takes place between a multitude of actors. Here, the primary added value lies in the co-creation of knowledge between different stakeholders. In today's multipolar world, the challenges faced by societies are increasingly interlinked (e.g. climate change, energy shortage and food insecurity) and international organisations struggle to make an impact. The internet and social networks have introduced radically new ways of producing knowledge. The ability to share ideas openly enables global communities to learn and share experiences. This can be organized as a so-called peer production – a decentralized, collaborative and non-proprietary process of knowledge and sharing under liberal license regimes[63]. Co-created knowledge is quicker, more suitable to diverse usage forms and more attuned to rapidly spreading technical and social innovations. Global collaboration allows interlinked problems to be solved quickly, striking a balance between respecting the intellectual property of corporations and institutions and giving communities access to advanced knowledge with fair and just conditions for everyone.

Enhanced connectivity between different stakeholders fosters such processes of voluntary interaction and exchange while at the same time being supported by them. Enhanced connectivity can be seen as a major added value of Knowledge Sharing on the societal level. The ability or likelihood of acting increases, due to new or improved relationships, a greater affinity and improved trust. This may lead not only to an increased network density, but can ideally help to create an increased sense of belonging[64]. Unexpected productivity can occur in the presence of cultural non-understanding when the differences between social groups is not seen as a nuisance but rather a chance to question the habits of the in-group[65]. Connectivity between stakeholders within and between societies is also strengthened through the existence of semi-public spaces where partners can address issues openly (including their own failures) that they probably would not usually state in public. Semi-public spaces are characterized by the fact that there is neither complete privacy, nor complete transparency. These are spaces par excellence for Knowledge Sharing[66]. By providing space, interactive methods

---

63   For the example of Wikipedia see: Seibold 2014.
64   World Bank 2015a: 20ff.
65   Piefer et al. 2015: 9.
66   Piefer et al. 2015: 13.

and structures for the co-creation of knowledge, a change in attitude can be reached on societal level, which might express itself through an improved consensus between different stakeholders.

Measurement of the Added Value of Knowledge Sharing

The measurement of the added value of Knowledge Sharing is necessary for development practitioners and decision makers to know whether activities are "achieving the intended results [...] and, if not, what corrective actions are needed"[67]. For this reason, monitoring and evaluation has become a key topic for mutual learning and studies in the Global Partnership on Knowledge Sharing[68].

Monitoring and evaluation tasks for Knowledge Sharing are principally the same as for any Monitoring & Evalution (M&E) activities in development programs and projects, therefore the basic studies and institutional set-ups on that issue will not be further discussed here. Nevertheless, there are some aspects to be kept in mind for the specific needs of Knowledge Sharing. Generally, there is a distinction to be made between "quantitative – 'hard' indicators such as how often users are accessing, contributing to, or using the knowledge assets and sharing processes" and "qualitative, 'soft' measures produced by asking people about their attitudes toward the activity"[69]. In their study on measurements of the value added in trilateral cooperation, a more focused, but closely related issue within the field of new cooperation forms, Nadine Piefer, Ulrich Müller and Claudia Taylor[70] make the same observation: In "current discussions on trilateral cooperation, the value added is perceived as part of 'soft factors' and 'on top' of the main results." The main results are generally achieved through developmental work in the beneficiary country. Nevertheless, they argue that the factors determining the value added by trilateral cooperation should also be considered as "hard" factors. Therefore[71], they call for "a new art of measuring". Following this advice, the same can be applied to the measurement of the added value of Knowledge Sharing. With Knowledge Sharing being an integral part of development programs and projects, not only their direct

---

67   Janus 2016: 109.
68   GPKS 2016: 1.
69   Janus 2016: 109.
70   Piefer et al. 2015: 7.
71   Ibid.: 22.

development effects in the beneficiary country should be measured as "hard" factors, but also the personal, organisational and societal improvements achieved among all partners, such as trust building, connectivity or co-creation.

This calls for new sets of quantitative and qualitative indicators that enable measurement of such benefits beyond the mere count of clicks and attendants in workshops. In this regard, Steffen Janus[72] suggests one possible set of indicators for Knowledge Sharing[73]. The OECD DAC in 2017 elaborated a draft alternative set of indicators, as a follow-up to an international meeting on triangular co-operation in Lisbon in 2016 and based on working with the before mentioned study of Nadine Piefer, Ulrich Müller and Claudia Taylor[74], here again related to the closely comparable needs of triangular cooperation[75].

Figure 3: Indicators for measuring Knowledge Sharing (World Bank)

Intermediate-outcome indicators
• Improved collaboration among staff or between departments
• Dedicated budget for knowledge and learning instituted
• New or adapted knowledge and learning governance established
• Incentive mechanisms for open peer learning instituted
• Extended/more effective domestic and international partnerships established
• Improved capabilities to conduct result-oriented and relevant Knowledge Sharing
Result indicators
• Solutions scaled-up at the organisational level
• Solutions replicated domestically or internationally
• Improved and/or higher quality service delivery achieved
• More innovations registered or implemented
• Efficiencies gained in core operations
• Higher visibility of client's knowledge-sharing capacity at domestic and international levels

Source: Janus 2016

---

72   Janus 2016: 110.
73   See Figure 3.
74   Piefer et al. 2015.
75   See Figure 4.

Figure 4: Draft toolkit for formulating indicators to take account of the value-added of triangular co-operation (OECD)

Draft indicators to measure ownership and horizontal partnerships (cross-cutting to all other areas)
• Proportion of all partners feeling valued (%) • Proportion of partners who felt they could influence the process (%) • Proportion of tasks by partner involved in the project (%) • Dollar value of all contributions (e.g. in-kind, staff time, guarantees) by each partner ($) • Partners trust each other with administering joint funds (yes/no) • Partners trust each other with other resources (yes/no) • Example of concrete joint fund/resource administration (yes/no) • Proportion of partners who state that they trust advice from other members (%) • Share of major project decisions taken jointly (%) • Examples of project ideas being presented by the beneficiary partner (yes/no; no.) • Examples of joint experiences presented at the national or international level (yes/no; no.) • Examples of adapted technology and new equipment being used (yes/no; no.) • Examples of activities that took place in other areas (e.g. trade, culture, etc.) following the project (yes/no; no.)
Draft indicators to measure complementarity
• Examples that show the specific expertise/technology that partners bring into the project are acknowledged by at least two participants (no.) • Value for money: ratio of local vs. external experts (total cost and time) • Examples showing the complementarity between the needed capacities and expected exchange of experiences in the project (no.) • Examples of flexibility, adaptation and changes during the project lifespan (yes/no; no.) • Proportion of partners that feel that based on the project experience they will adapt their mechanisms of development co-operation in the future (%) • Examples that acknowledge/incorporate innovations that were generated from pooling expertise and resources of all partners (no.)

• Evidence of change/adaptation of development co-operation mechanisms (yes/no)
Draft indicators to measure Knowledge Sharing and joint learning
• Examples that illustrate systematic Knowledge Sharing (yes/no; no.) • Perception of partners that knowledge is shared systematically (yes/no) • Proportion of partners that perceive that they are learning from the other partners (%) • Examples of joint learning (yes/no; no.) • Examples of concrete knowledge transfer (yes/no; no.) • Dollar value of budget spent on facilitating joint learning ($) • Examples where the results of a joint learning process are being applied in the project (yes/no; no.) • Project participants report examples of improvements in their individual performance in executing their daily duties as a result of joint learning and knowledge-sharing initiatives (no.) • Evidence/examples that lessons learned/capacity developed is feeding into another activity/future project • Share of partners that feel their capacities have been strengthened (%; no.) • Share of partners that apply their newly acquired capacities and skills in the project (%; no.) • Proportion of partners who feel that the project experience has contributed to changes in their institutions (%)
Draft indicators to measure co-creating development solutions
• Examples and share of solutions to development challenges that have been found jointly by the partners involved (%; no.) • Examples capturing local knowledge to achieve project goals (yes/no; no.) • Number of tools, systems and technology adapted from exchanges in the triangular co-operation project (no.) • Examples of adapted tools/systems presented in the triangular co-operation project (no.) • Examples of internal rules and regulations that are changed (yes/no; no.) • Examples of policies that are changed (yes/no; no.)
Draft indicators to measure scaling-up and sustainability
• Dollar value of additional resources mobilised ($)

• Number of partnership agreements with external partners (no.) while the project is running • Perception of innovation in setting up additional partnerships (yes/no) • Examples of planned follow-up activities designed and implemented up to x months after project completion (no.; yes/no) • Number of post-project follow-up activities based on the recommendations from the monitoring and evaluation reports (no.) • Examples of (continued) co-operation beyond the project duration (yes/no; no.)
Draft indicators to measure achieving global development goals
• Examples of joint positions taken in multilateral policy fora (yes/no; no.) • Examples of joint actions at the UN, regional and other bodies where all partners are members (yes/no; no.) • Diversity of the actors involved (no. of different types of partners, e.g. civil society, private sector) • Evidence that project outcomes are aligned to SDGs at target level (yes/no; no.) • Examples of shifts from short-term development co-operation to a long-term vision of development partnership (yes/no; no.)

Source: OECD 2017

Both lists provide a lot of interesting "food for thought" and some of the proposed indicators are already being used in the design of development projects and programs. However, no systematic analysis of experiences using these indicators has yet been carried out. For that purpose, the baseline of experience in the use of the proposed indicators must be broadened in order to provide a basis for introducing them more systematically in standard monitoring and evaluation procedures.

Conclusion

There is a wide range and a great variety of Knowledge Sharing experiences in Latin America. The broad interest by many different groups of actors in this mode of cooperation shows that its benefits are not expected to be easily achieved through other means of cooperation. In describing these benefits, associating Knowledge Sharing only with personal learning falls far short of the fuller picture. Knowledge Sharing also takes place between organisations and societies. The particular ways learning occurs at the level of these entities are strongly linked with the development of processes and regulations. There are also interesting interrelations between the learning of persons, organisations and societies, such as when persons start to create new organisational processes or when societies change the overall conditions and incentives for learning.

On the other hand, the term Knowledge Sharing itself seems somehow misleading because it concerns far more than just knowledge. A lot can also be shared in terms of ability and, perhaps even more importantly, in terms of attitude. In the development of personal, organisational and societal competences knowledge, ability and attitude work hand in hand and mutually reinforce each other.

When the perspectives of person, organisation and society on the one hand and knowledge, ability and attitude on the other are combined, it is possible to identify a range of different ways in which Knowledge Sharing gives added value. This may also provide inspiration for improved measurement of the added value of Knowledge Sharing. Some possible indicators have already been proposed. It is important to gain experiences with the application of these indicators in order to strengthen the debate on the added value of Knowledge Sharing.

Bibliography

AMEXCID/JICA (2012): Catálogo de Capacidades Mexicanas de Cooperación Internacional para el Desarrollo. Accessible under: https://www.gob.mx/cms/uploads/attachment/file/109702/catalogo-de-capacidades-mexicanas-de-cid-2012.pdf (10.31.2017).

Arnold, Rolf (2010): Selbstbildung, Schneider Verlag, Baltsmannsweiler.

Arnold, Rolf (2012): Ermöglichen, Schneider Verlag, Baltmannsweiler.

Borbolla Compean, Daniela (2014): La construcción institucional de la Agencia Mexicana de Cooperación Internacional para el Desarrollo, Revista Mexicana de Política Exterior, Vol. 102(2014), pp. 55-70.

Bukowitz, Wendi R./Williams, Ruth L. (1999): The Knowledge Management Fieldbook, Financial Times, Prentice Hall, Upper Saddle River, New Jersey.

Drucker, Peter F. (1993): Post-Capitalist Society, Butterworth Heinemann, Oxford.

Erpenbeck, John/Sauter, Werner (2013): So werden wir lernen. Kompetenzentwicklung in einer Welt fühlender Computer, kluger Wolken und sinnsuchender Netze, Springer, Heidelberg.

Erpenbeck, John/Rosenstiel, Lutz von (eds.) (2007): Handbuch Kompetenzmessung. Erkennen, verstehen und bewerten von Kompetenzen in der betrieblichen, pädagogischen und psychologischen Praxis, 2nd edition, Schäffer-Poeschel, Stuttgart, pp. XVII-XLVI.

Giddens, Anthony (1995): Die Konstitution der Gesellschaft. Grundzüge einer Theorie der Strukturierung, 2nd edition, Campus Frankfurt/Main, New York.

GIZ (Deutsche Gesellschaft für Internationale Zusammenarbeit) (2015): Cooperation Management for Practitioners - Managing Social Change with Capacity WORKS. Springer Gabler, Wiesbaden.

GPKS (Global Partnership on Knowledge Sharing) (2016): Towards Action on Country-led Solutions for Sustainable Development. Perspectives from the first meeting of the Global Partnership on Knowledge Sharing, World Bank. Accessible under: https://www.knowledgesharingfordev.org/Data/wbi/wbicms/files/drupal-acquia/wbi/document_repository/20160414_summary_gpks_meeting.pdf (05.01.2017).

Gobierno de México (2011): Ley de Cooperación Internacional para el Desarrollo (LCID).

Hannig, Alfred/Leifheit, Maren/Lázaro Rüther, Lena (2014): The Alliance for Financial Inclusion. Bringing Smart Policies to Life, in: Lázaro Rüther, Lena/Ayala Martínez, Citlali/Müller, Ulrich (eds.): Global Funds and Networks. Narrowing the Gap between Global Policies and National Implementation, Nomos, Baden-Baden, pp. 199-208.

Janus, Steffen Soulejman (2016): Becoming a Knowledge-Sharing Organisation. A Handbook for Scaling Up Solutions through Knowledge Capturing and Sharing, World Bank, Washington D.C.

Jonas, Klaus/Stroebe, Wolfgang/Hewstone, Miles (2014): Sozialpsychologie, Springer, Berlin.

Kath, Joachim (2016): SinnNavi 2 Politische Haltung. Wissen Kompakt, epubli, Berlin.

Krewer, Bernd/Uhlmann, Adelheid (2015): Models for Human Capacity Development. Didactics Concept of the Academy for International Cooperation, Deutsche Gesellschaft für Internationale Zusammenarbeit, Bonn.

Leutner, Jana/Rösch, Michael (2014): Global Networks. Extractive Industries Transparency Initiative, in: Lázaro Rüther, Lena/Ayala Martínez, Citlali/Müller, Ulrich (eds.): Global Funds and Networks. Narrowing the Gap between Global Policies and National Implementation, Nomos, Baden-Baden, pp. 209-220.

OECD-DAC (Organisation for Economic Co-operation and Development – Development Assistance Committee) (2017): Tool 2. Formulating indicators to take account of the value-added of triangular co-operation. Toolkit for identifying, monitoring and evaluating the value-added of triangular co-operation. Draft.

OECD-DAC (Organisation for Economic Co-operation and Development – Development Assistance Committee) (2016): Converged Statistical Reporting Directives for the Creditor Reporting System (CRS) and the Annual DAC Questionaire. Accessible under: http://www.oecd.org/dac/financing-sustainable-development/development-finance-standards/ (03.21.2017).

Paulin, Dan/Suneson, Kaj (2012): Knowledge Transfer, Knowledge Sharing and Knowledge Barriers – Three Blurry Terms in KM, The Electronic Journal of Knowledge Management, Vol 10(1), pp.81-91.

Pérez Pineda, Jorge Antonio/Ayala Martínez, Citlali/De la O Lopez, Felipe (2015): Diagnóstico sobre la cooperación internacional para el desarrollo en México 2014-2015, Instituto Mora.

Perloff, Richard M. (2016): The Dynamics of Persuasion. Communication and Attitudes in the Twenty-First Century, 2nd edition, Routledge, London.

Piefer, Nadine/Müller, Ulrich/Taylor, Claudia (2015): Exploring Ways Towards Measuring the Value Add in Trilateral Cooperation. With inputs from: Pavlina Buzkova, Christian Gmelin, Marton Kocsev, Stefan Pennig, Joachim Vogt, Ulrike Wissler, and Gesa Ziemer. GIZ internal document.

Sauter, Werner/Scholz, Christiana (2015): Von der Personalentwicklung zur Lernbegleitung, Springer, Wiesbaden.

Sauter, Werner/Staudt, Franz-Peter (2016): Strategisches Kompetenzmanagement 2.0, Springer, Wiesbaden.

Schütz, Alfred/Luckmann, Thomas (1994): Strukturen der Lebenswelt, Vol. 2, 3rd edition, Suhrkamp, Frankfurt am Main.

Seibold, Balthas (2014): Learning by Sharing. How global communities cultivate skills and capacity through peer-production of knowledge, in: GIZ (ed.): 10 trends in open innovation. How to leverage social media for new forms of cooperation. Accessible under: http://10innovations.alumniportal.com/ (10.31.2017).

Serban, Andreea M./Luan, Jing (2002): Overview of Knowledge Management, New Directions for Institutional Research, 2002(113), pp. 5-16.

United Nations (2015): Transforming our World. The 2030 Agenda for Sustainable Development. Resolution adopted by the General Assembly on 25 September 2015. Accessible under: https://sustainabledevelopment.un.org/post2015/transformingourworld (03.05.2017).

Vega, Bernadette (2014): Country Study Mexico, in: Piefer, Nadine: Experiences of Middle-Income Countries in International Development Cooperation. Study prepared for Agencia Mexicana de Cooperación Internacional para el Desarrollo (AMEXCID) and Deutsche Gesellschaft für Internationale Zusammenarbeit (GIZ), GIZ, Bonn/Eschborn.

Werlen, Benno (1995): Konzeptionen sozialer Wirklichkeit und geographische Sozialforschung, in: Matznetter, Walter (ed.): Geographie und Gesellschaftstheorie. Referate im Rahmen des „Anglo-Austrian Seminar on Geography and Social Theory" in Zell am Moos, Oberösterreich, Beiträge zur Bevölkerungs- und Sozialgeographie, Bd. 3, Institut für Geographie der Universität Wien, Wien.

World Bank (2015a): The Art of Knowledge Exchange. A Results-Focused Planning Guide for Development Practitioners, 2nd edition, World Bank, Washington DC. Accessible under: https://openknowledge.worldbank.org/bitstream/handle/10986/11983/74263.pdf?sequence=1&isAllowed=y (05.23.2017).

World Bank (2015b): Scaling up Knowledge Sharing for development. A working paper for the G-20 development working group, Pillar 9, World Bank Group, Washington, D.C. Accessible under: http://documents.worldbank.org/curated/en/4291114681 88931035/Scaling-up-knowledge-sharing-for-development-a-working-paper-for-the-G-20-development-working-group-pillar-nine (11.01.2017).

Zapf, Wolfgang (1989): Über soziale Innovationen, in: Soziale Welt, Vol. 40(1-2), pp. 170-183.

Ziemer, Gesa (2013): Komplizenschaft. Neue Perspektiven auf Kollektivität, Transcript, Bielefeld.

Extractive Industries and Knowledge Sharing: Experiences from Ecuador through the Experts' Network Evidence and Lessons from Latin America (ELLA)

Marcela Morales Hidalgo and Melani Peláez Jara

Introduction

In September of 2015, the international community agreed upon the 2030 Agenda for Sustainable Development, a universal agenda which outlines the path towards achieving the 17 Sustainable Development Goals (SDG) and their 169 targets[1]. This new agenda, which builds on the Millennium Development Goals (MDGs), is without doubt the international community's most ambitious collective action plan ever. Achieving these goals will only be possible by engaging and cooperating with all relevant and possible stakeholders. In the endeavour towards the MDGs, international development cooperation underwent a process of change from traditional North-South "linear transfer" paradigms, to more participative and multi-stakeholder modes and strategies of collaboration. These relatively new modes of cooperation acknowledge the need to foster horizontal activities, Knowledge Sharing and exchange tools, South-South dialogue spaces, global and local networks of experts, etc.

During the last decade, Latin American and Caribbean (LAC) countries have achieved significant progress at several levels: poverty reduction, economic growth, gender equality, environmental protection, etc. Many LAC economies are now in a position to share their lessons, challenges, and experiences with other countries and regions. This is where the aforementioned new modes of cooperation play an important role, not only for public entities cooperating at a government level, but also for the private sector, non-profit, academic, and civil-society organisations. Non-governmental organisations and think tanks in particular are among those who can profit

---

1   United Nations General Assembly 2015.

the most from formats such as Knowledge Sharing activities in networks of experts and professionals[2].

This chapter aims to depict the experiences of Grupo FARO (Foundation for the Advance of Reforms and Opportunities), the Ecuadorian research partner of the Evidence and Lessons from Latin America program (ELLA), specifically in researching extractive industries and transparency. Based on the analysis of interviews with partners of the project, relevant literature including documents of the project, and a glance through Grupo FARO's own experiences, this short case study seeks to contribute a South American and practical perspective on Knowledge Sharing among experts' networks. It does not aim to provide an in-depth theoretical understanding of Knowledge Sharing in experts' networks. It rather seeks to contribute to closing the literature gap on practical experiences from Ecuador and Latin America around this topic, bearing some scholarly points of view on Knowledge Sharing in advocacy networks and epistemic communities.

We structured this chapter as follows: in the second section we will briefly highlight the relevance and similarities of advocacy networks and epistemic communities for understanding Knowledge Sharing activities. In the third section we will depict Grupo FARO and its experience as part of the ELLA program, while in the fourth section we will focus on the Ecuadorian-Ugandan sharing experience in extractive industries. The final section will emphasize on the lessons learned and the challenges ahead of organisations like Grupo FARO and networks like ELLA.

Knowledge in advocacy networks and epistemic communities

When it comes to informing policy makers on pressing issues, the collaboration between scientists, experts, and practitioners is key. However, this collaboration is conditioned to the context of the policy in question, the stakeholders involved, among other factors. Yet, the most important aspect of this collaboration is perhaps the knowledge and expertise that is generated and shared among stakeholders. The study of these interactions and learning processes at the global and local level has drawn the attention of scholars from different disciplines and has raised questions on how to better canalize knowledge to improve decision making at the policy making level. In this framework, networks of experts and researchers' networks have raised as promising spaces to achieve these goals.

---

2   Haas 1992.

Mutual learning and Knowledge Sharing have been included as key elements in different network typologies. In this brief theoretical review, we will focus on two types of experts' networks for Knowledge Sharing: transnational advocacy networks and epistemic communities. These two types of networks can help us understand the work and evolution of research centres like Grupo FARO in Ecuador. As other think tanks in Latin America, Grupo FARO transitioned from a civil society organisation focused on research and advocacy at the national and local level to an organisation with a regional focus and strong ties with experts and networks in the global south.

Margaret Keck and Kathryn Sikkink[3] emphasize the importance of international networks of experts, or activists, organized under common values and motivations in policy processes and societal change. These networks, also called transnational advocacy networks, can become spaces where different actors bring norms and discourses into policy debate, while taking part in or triggering mutual learning processes that entail more than the mere diffusion of ideas and practices. Such networks of experts seek mutual influence and transformation through the exchange of each network member's existing and new ideas and values[4]. This shared learning process amongst different stakeholders constitutes one of the core characteristics of transnational advocacy networks, where the spread of knowledge, experiences, and certain discourses happen in a horizontal and peer environment[5]. Advocacy networks are inclusive, in the sense that they include all types of stakeholders, from engaged citizens, local activists, to scientific experts that share their beliefs and values, and who are willing to advocate for them.

Unlike advocacy networks, in epistemic communities the participating actors are academic or scientific experts in any discipline, with some degree of (even direct) access to decision making actors or circles, therefore making them tacitly exclusive[6]. The members of an epistemic community also share certain principles and causal beliefs, standards and methods to validate knowledge in their domain of expertise, and common Knowledge Sharing practices among peers and with other policy actors[7]. By underlining

---

3   Keck/Sikkink 1999.
4   Ibid.; Stone 2002.
5   Keck/Sikkink 1999; Lázaro et al. 2014.
6   Stone 2001; Stone 2002.
7   Haas 1992; Haas 2000.

their characteristic expertise in both the scientific method and technical content, epistemic communities seek to demarcate themselves from governmental interests, even though close collaboration with decision makers is key for their existence as networks[8].

Advocacy networks depend as much as epistemic communities on how they deploy their knowledge generation and sharing activities, in order to achieve the impact such networks aim for. Yet, practical cases of experts' networks rarely correspond to one single specific typology – they are rather hybrids. We argue that the case of Grupo FARO and its Knowledge Sharing activities with peers from Africa and other regions in the context of ELLA can be understood from the perspective of both an advocacy network and an epistemic community, as we will explain further on.

From think-tanks to think-nets: Grupo FARO's experience generating knowledge through networks

Grupo FARO is an Ecuadorian research and advocacy centre that is mostly concerned with the implementation of projects and citizen-lead initiatives. According to the organisation's self-stated mission, Grupo FARO supports the State, the private sector and civil society to promote a more democratic, efficient and participative public policy process. In these lines, Grupo FARO aims to strengthen the public sphere; a space where the government, the civil society and the private sector can identify common challenges and generate innovative solutions through collective action[9].

In recent years, Grupo FARO has worked on topics related to education, health, budget transparency, extractive industries, natural resources, knowledge management, among others. The thematic focus of the organisation is accompanied by transversal activities that hold the work of the organisation together:

- Capacity building to encourage and strengthen the State, the private sector and the civil society's capacity to actively participate in the public sphere.
- Research aimed at the generation of knowledge to respond to policy debates and policy needs.
- Creation of learning spaces to encourage the exchange and promotion of good practices among stakeholders.
- Creation of networks to support Grupo FARO's work on a local, national, and regional scale.

---

8   Stone 2002; Stone 2008.
9   Grupo FARO 2016b.

Research and knowledge management are two of the most important aspects of Grupo FARO's approach to public policy. In this regard, and in order to answer to Ecuador's changing political environment, in 2013 Grupo FARO adopted a renewed institutional research and knowledge management policy[10]. This institutional change was a response to the presence of a stronger State with the capacity to design and formulate public policy.

It is important to keep in mind that by the time Grupo FARO was founded in 2004, the country was going through one of the most politically troubled periods in its history. Between 2000 and 2007, Ecuador had 3 presidents in office. Given that the usual presidential mandate lasts 4 years, this period is considered as one of high political instability and polarisation[11]. Grupo FARO as other civil society actors emerged as an initiative to promote dialogue and to articulate the efforts of key actors in a highly fragmented political scenario with an institutionally weak State[12]. During this period, Grupo FARO's purpose was to position itself as a producer of research and knowledge to inform better decision making at the policy level[13].

After 2007, the State progressively regained stability in its central role supported by an improvement in the overall economic situation[14]. In this scenario, civil society organisations (CSOs) had to review their roles and the spaces in which they had been operating[15]. Additionally, under the Correa Administration[16] (especially after 2013), the scope of regulation on CSOs underwent significant transformations[17] with a correspondingly major impact and constraints on the activities they performed[18]. As the Ecuadorian State became stronger and increased its institutional capacity to design and implement public policy, the tasks of research and knowledge generation provided by think tanks needed to go beyond monitoring and social vigilance. They needed to focus more on the generation of knowledge that

---

10   Grupo FARO 2013.
11   International Crisis Group 2007.
12   Ortiz 2012.
13   Grupo FARO 2013.
14   Recalde 2014.
15   Grupo FARO 2013.
16   Rafael Correa was President of Ecuador until 2017. He was elected for the first time in 2007 and was reelected in 2013, becoming the longest-serving Ecuadorian president in three decades.
17   CEOSC 2016.
18   Conaghan 2016.

could contribute to policy generation, and applied knowledge to enrich the public debate[19].

Against this backdrop, Grupo FARO identified the need to rethink its approach to research and knowledge generation. In 2013, Grupo FARO's Executive Board approved a new institutional research policy aimed at:

- Generating rigorous and independent research to respond to the needs of an institutionally and technically stronger State.
- Increasing opportunities to inform and influence public policy debate.
- Positioning Grupo FARO's work in the public sphere and strengthening its organisational identity.

Within these guidelines, Grupo FARO redefined its identity as a civil society organisation that generates independent applied research and knowledge to inform public policy; and an independent public policy centre that seeks to inform and influence policy debate. To portray this situation, Figure 1 shows Grupo FARO's scope and mode of work (Mendizabal, 2010).

---

19   CEOSC 2016.

Figure 1: Grupo FARO's scope and mode of work

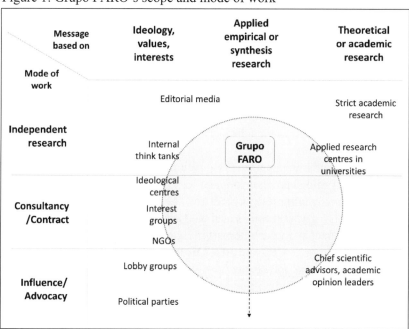

Source: Adapted from Mendizabal 2010.

This diagram places Grupo FARO's work within the realm of think tanks (light grey sphere): somewhere in-between ideologically driven advocacy and independent theoretical research, or from the theoretical perspective mentioned above, between the characteristics of an advocacy network organisation and those of an epistemic community organisation. Grupo FARO's mode of work is located closer to the independent research realm based on applied or empirical research. By balancing ideologically driven and theoretically driven work, the organisation is better able to position itself as an independent entity that can present itself as a desirable and useful partner for both academics and advocates[20]. Grupo FARO's work sphere does seek to encompass a certain degree of influence or advocacy. However, unlike NGOs or interest groups focused on campaigns that are purely ideologically driven, Grupo FARO's advocacy work constantly strives to

---

20   Mendizabal 2010.

base its work on methodologically sound and independent applied research (hence the arrow).

To bring this research and knowledge approach into practice, Grupo FARO collaborates with networks of organisations that produce knowledge and are committed to common projects[21]. Collaborative networks for knowledge generation have the potential to transform think tanks into think-nets[22]. In order to pursue this endeavour, Grupo FARO is currently a member of networks formed by other CSOs at the national and regional level. Some of these networks include:

- Evidence and Lessons from Latin America (ELLA). This initiative aims to identify and share development lessons between Latin America and Africa by engaging research centres from both regions in an exchange that entails research and learning. Grupo FARO participates in this learning space with a counterpart in Uganda (ACODE). The partnership between Grupo FARO and ACODE focuses on the topic of local content in the oil and gas sector[23].
- Latin American Network for Public Policy Research (ILAIPP). ILAIPP is a collaborative effort of research centres from several countries in Central and South America to influence public policy debate and development in the region. According to its mission, ILAIPP seeks to be recognized as a sharing and learning space for Latin American think tanks[24]. Grupo FARO is among the organisations that are part of this network.
- Latin American Network for Extractives Industries (RLIE). RLIE was born to answer to the concerns of civil society organisations in the region on the impact of extractive industries in Latin America. This network encompasses 13 CSOs that collaboratively generate debate and research on topics such as revenue management, transparency, social conflicts, etc.[25].
- Ecuadorian Confederation of Civil Society Organisations (CEOSC). This space seeks to generate dialogue between CSOs and other public actors (the state, universities, international cooperation, etc.) on issues

---

21   Bellettini 2013.
22   Grupo FARO 2013.
23   ELLA 2016b.
24   ILAIPP 2016.
25   RLIE 2016.

related to transparency, democracy, and participation. The CEOSC was conceived as a constructive approach towards Presidential Decree 982 that regulated CSO activities in Ecuador[26]. Grupo FARO was among the founding organisations of this network. In 2012, 102 organisations joined this initiative[27].

Grupo FARO's involvement in these networks provides the organisation with the opportunity to engage in mutual learning processes with other think tanks and CSOs, and to identify further areas of collaboration. These areas of collaboration include capacity building spaces, funding opportunities and increased potential for impact and visibility. As spaces to generate research and knowledge, networks also present the opportunity for organisations like Grupo FARO and its peers to position themselves as experts in different fields, increasing its influence at the national and local level.

This has been the case with Grupo FARO's Extractive Industries Program (EIP), through its participation in both the Latin American Network for Extractive Industries (RLIE) and Evidence and Lessons from Latin America (ELLA). Grupo FARO's Extractive Industries Program has been one of the most successful within the organisation, and its success has been measured in terms of the organisation's ability to transform local and national expertise into regional and inter-regional experience.

Grupo FARO's work related to the extractive industries in Ecuador has mainly been focused on the promotion of transparency in the oil and mining sector. Due to the strategic importance that the extractive industries have in Ecuador, Grupo FARO has managed to position itself as a connection between the State and other civil society actors[28]. Since its creation in 2009, the Extractive Industries Program has been active at the local level (mostly in oil producing regions and communities) where there has been greater availability of opportunities to work directly with policy makers and citizen-led organisations[29]. This experience has been of importance for the mutual learning process together with peers of the RLIE and ELLA.

After joining the Latin American Network for Extractive Industries (RLIE), the EIP's activities moved to a higher level by incorporating a regional and a comparative perspective into the mostly locally based work the program had been doing until then. In this scenario, another very important

---

26   CEOSC 2016.
27   Ibid.
28   Grupo FARO 2016a.
29   Grupo FARO 2016a.

benefit was the generation of mutual learning spaces, where fellow CSOs can share their experiences and common challenges. Figure 2 explains this dynamic.

Figure 2: Grupo FARO's Extractive Industries Program and its interaction with the Latin American Network for Extractive Industries (RLIE) and Evidence and Lessons from Latin America (ELLA)

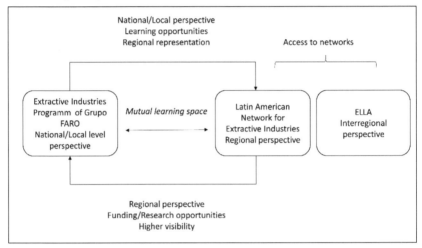

Source: Created by the authors.

In terms of research and knowledge generation, access to specialized networks (in this case extractive industries networks), had an impact or feedback effect on the Extractive Industries Program's approach towards research. EIP's nationally/locally based approach during its first years translated into descriptive knowledge products mostly oriented to the reporting and explanation of sectoral laws, contracts and economic indicators of the extractive sector in Ecuador[30]. While the adoption of comparative perspectives into its knowledge generation processes was not necessarily a direct consequence of the organisation's participation in the RLIE, it was certainly a related factor. The existence of funding opportunities and the availability of skills development spaces to generate multi-country and comparative research facilitated the adoption of this approach.

Access to networks such as the RLIE also facilitated the identification and eventual participation by Grupo FARO and its Extractive Industries

---

30   Ibid.

Program in other expert networks such as ELLA, where the focus of the knowledge generation process is interregional. This also represented another step forward in recognizing Latin America's value as a source of knowledge and experience on a range of development topics.

An Ecuadorian-Ugandan sharing experience: Transforming National Expertise into Regionally Relevant Knowledge through the ELLA Initiative

The research, exchange and learning program Evidence and Lessons from Latin America (ELLA) is an initiative funded in 2009 by the Department for International Development of the United Kingdom (DFID)[31]. ELLA is managed by the international NGO Practical Action Latin America (PAC) and is supported by the Institute of Development Studies (IDS). The second phase of this program, which started in 2014 and is to be funded until 2017, seeks to enable African and Latin American actors to be involved in economic, environmental and governance policy making to share, debate, and learn about experiences from Latin American peers. This program targets not only decision makers, but also all other relevant experts and practitioners actively shaping and influencing the policy field, including research centres, think tanks, and CSOs.

The current phase, also called ELLA 2, is based on the following principles[32]:

- Work with research centres committed to rigorous research and evidence based policy making.
- Focus on research that is relevant for policy making and development agendas.
- Commit to rigorous and comparative research that acknowledges context and good academic standards.
- Generate practical evidence and output that produces practical recommendations and lessons for decision makers and social actors.
- Produce learning processes based on interregional exchange opportunities that concentrate on adapting and understanding research conclusions.
- Partake in action-oriented activities that seek to motivate policy-makers to implement lessons learned on policies.

---

31   DFID n.d.
32   ELLA 2015.

The current ELLA phase has both a geographic and a thematic focus: evidence and lessons learned on environmental management, governance and economic development from Latin America that can be shared and adapted in Africa. Twelve research centres in Colombia, Ecuador, Peru, Argentina, El Salvador, Mexico[33], South Africa, Kenya, Uganda, Nigeria and Ghana are pursuing collaborative research on[34]:

- Informality and inclusive growth
- Land tenure in pastoralist societies
- Oil and gas local content
- Accountability of the executive to legislative bodies
- Domestic violence.

Grupo FARO joined the ELLA Initiative in October 2014 after a selection process led by Practical Action (PAC) in Peru and the Institute for Development Studies (IDS) in the University of Sussex. Research centres in Africa and Latin America were asked to submit a research proposal based on their interests and expertise. Based on the same criteria, centres in both regions were paired so they could conduct comparative research and participate in a mutual learning process on the selected topic.

Grupo FARO was matched with the Ugandan research centre ACODE (Advocates Coalition for Development and Environment). Both organisations identified the extractive sector (specifically the oil and gas sector) to be of mutual interest. In the case of Latin America, the region has already extensive experience in the extraction of natural resources, both in technical and policy related aspects. This contrasted with the African case that has a considerably younger sector and less experience in the field[35]. Among the vast array of topics within natural resource management, local content[36] was

---

33   Ayala 2014.
34   ELLA 2016a.
35   Morales et al. 2016.
36   Local content is defined as the extent to which the output of the extractive industry sector generates further benefits to the domestic economy beyond direct contributions through productive linkages with other sectors (Tordo/Anouti 2013). These linkages are created when the oil and gas industry purchases inputs that are supplied domestically instead of importing them, hires domestic labour or promotes skills development and knowledge transfer (Auty 2006; Heum et al. 2003).

selected as the focus of the exchange between Latin American Grupo FARO and African ACODE.

Once the research centres were paired, the ELLA Initiative expected the centres to engage in a series of activities anchored in the generation and sharing of knowledge: the generation of policy-relevant knowledge, and the identification of good lessons and practices from Africa and Latin America related to the topic of local content in the oil and gas sector.

The specific areas of work within ELLA 2 include:

- Research Papers Series. Research is one of the main knowledge outputs of ELLA 2. Over two years (2014-2016), Grupo FARO and ACODE independently and jointly conducted regional and comparative research on local content practices in Africa and Latin America. The knowledge products included:
- One Design and Methods Paper. This paper was developed jointly between Grupo FARO and ACODE and establishes the methodological approach for the regional evidence papers and comparative evidence paper.
- Two Regional Evidence Papers (REP). Each centre conducted a regional analysis (Grupo FARO in Latin America and ACODE in Africa) on local content practices using similar methodologies and data in order to ensure further comparability. REPs highlight lessons identified in each region.
- One Comparative Evidence Paper (CEP). Both centres bring together the evidence identified in the REPs and based on a comparative exercise identify policy lessons related to local content that could be applied in Africa based on the Latin American experience.
- Learning Alliance (LEA). ELLA Learning Alliances bring together peers from across the global south to learn from one another, drawing on rigorous, evidence based research[37]. The main objective of the LEA is to share understanding and knowledge regarding lessons in tackling development challenges and to establish a community of practice among experts and practitioners from both regions.
- Communication Products. Based on the research paper series, the research uptake products include briefs, infographics and other materials meant to communicate the findings of the knowledge generation process to key audiences.

---

37   ELLA 2016b.

- Study Tour. Ten Learning Alliance (LEA) participants from Africa were selected to visit Ecuador to see first-hand the dynamics of the extractive sector in Latin America.

Figure 3. ELLA 2 knowledge generation and learning spaces

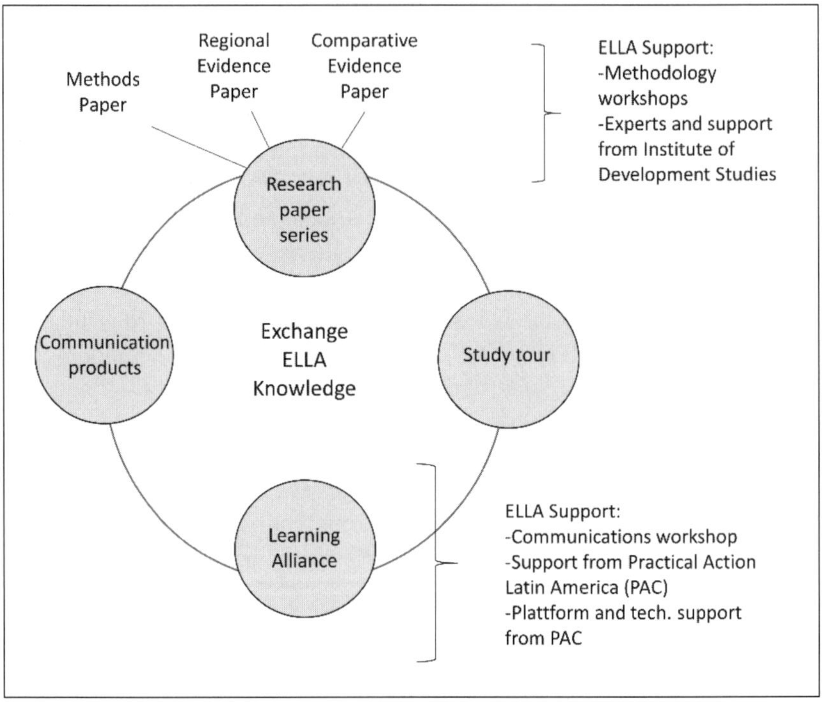

Source: Created by the authors based on ELLA 2016b.

For Grupo FARO and ACODE the participation in the ELLA Initiative is an opportunity to learn from peers on two levels. On the organisational level both organisations have been able to gain skills and experience on data validation methods, research methods, project management, quality control, communication and outreach. On the thematic level, both centres have been able to learn, not only about one another's regional particularities and technical expertise, but also about "fingertip expertise" that can be useful in the field[38].

---

38   Interview by Melani Peláez in 2016 with John Okiira about the experiences on the cooperation with ELLA and Grupo FARO.

This technical and organisational learning process has empowered both organisations in their local work as technical dialogue partners for policy makers, and as supporters of societal change. Their mutual learning process is also beneficial for their local, regional, and international networks, because it allows all participant members to share, test, and deploy knowledge, field skills, values, and common goals. At an international level, networks like ELLA also profit from stronger and more effective regional partners that share and spread common values and beliefs.

Lessons and Challenges

Regional networks are essential elements in generating perspectives from the global south. Regional platforms, despite having limited resources in some cases, have the ability and the potential to mobilize peers and partners to generate knowledge and create environments that are conducive to enhancing horizontal cooperation.

Regional dynamics in particular have the potential to solve or identify innovative approaches to common challenges and ease the collaborative generation of knowledge. However, the impact of such networks cannot only depend on mere research or mere advocacy. The development challenges that countries have ahead of them demand hybrid approaches to be solved. Researchers need to work closely with advocates and experts on the field in order to find solutions and adequate policy responses. In the same manner, countries and regions need to be able to identify and exploit their strengths in terms of knowledge and expertise and also identify what they can learn from others.

Grupo FARO′s participation in the ELLA Initiative, show the importance of developing hybrids between advocacy networks and epistemic communities. While ELLA promoted the generation of rigorous research and the involvement of academic institutions (IDS), it also highlighted the need to generate research that was relevant for policy making and that was communicated appropriately to relevant audiences. Academics, advocates and experts on the field were brought together to share and generate knowledge.

The main lesson that other civil society organisations can learn from the experience of Grupo FARO is to look for opportunities regionally: opportunities to learn, opportunities to share lessons, opportunities for skills development. Especially in settings where CSO′s activities have been limited due to political or financial circumstances, regional networks have the potential to strengthen organisation's presence and give them access to other sources of financing and institutional strengthening.

To achieve the agreed sustainable development goals, the sustainability of the mechanisms themselves and knowledge generated in networks should also be of concern to those moderating networks and the organisations participating in them. In the specific case of ELLA and its partners, and after the funding period of the initiative is over, it will be up to its members to capitalize on the experience generated during this process. In response to this situation, spaces such as ELLA's community of practice (Learning Alliances) are meant to maintain experts and practitioners from different areas in touch and to promote further communication after the initiative formally concludes. It is still to be defined whether such alternatives truly address community members' needs in the medium and long term.

Bibliography

Auty, Richard (2006): Mining enclave to economic catalyst. Large mineral projects in developing countries, Brown Journal of World Affairs, pp. 135-145.

Ayala Martínez, Citlali (2014): Evidence and Lessons in Latin America. Network for the Exchange of Good Practices in Public Policy, in: Lázaro Rüther, Lena/Ayala Martínez, Citlali/Müller, Ulrich (eds.): Global Funds and Networks. Narrowing the Gap between Global Policies and National Implementation, Nomos, Baden-Baden, pp. 249-262.

Bellettini, Orazio (2013): The future of think tanks in Latin America. Accessible under: https://onthinktanks.org/articles/orazio-bellettini-on-the-future-of-think-tanks-in-latin-america/ (10.19.2017).

CEOSC (Ecuadorian Confederation of Civil Society Organisations) (2016): History of the Confederation. Accesible under: http://www.confederacionecuatorianaosc.org/confederacion/confederacion/historia (10.19.2017).

Conaghan, Catherine (2016): Legal Norms and Civil Society Organisations. Lasa Forum.

DFID (Department for International Development of the United Kingdom) (n.d.): Research for Development- Project Record - Evidence and Lessons from Latin America (ELLA). Accessible under: http://r4d.dfid.gov.uk/Project/60739/ (01.04.2016).

ELLA (Evidence and Lessons from Latin America) (2015): Extrayendo Transparencia - ELLA 14-17 Infographic. Accessible under: http://extrayendotransparencia.grupofaro.org/wp-content/uploads/2015/10/150831-ELLA-Infographic-Sp.pdf (05.01.2016).

ELLA (Evidence and Lessons from Latin America) (2016a). ELLA - Programme Outline. Accessible under: http://ella.practicalaction.org/about/programme-outline/ (05.01.2016).

ELLA (Evidence and Lessons from Latin America) (2016b): Evidence and Lessons from Latin America (ELLA). Accessible under: http://ella.practicalaction.org/ (10.19.2017).

Grupo FARO (2013): El Nuevo Enfoque de Investigación de Grupo FARO, Grupo FARO, Quito.

Grupo FARO (2016a): Extrayendo Transparencia. Accessible under: http://extrayendo transparencia.grupofaro.org/ (10.19.2017).

Grupo FARO (2016b): ¿Quiénes somos? Accessible under: www.grupofaro.org (10.19.2017).

Haas, Peter (1992): Introduction. Epistemic Communities and International Policy Coordination, International Organisation, pp. 1-35.

Haas, Peter (2000): International Institutions and Social Learning in the Management of Global Environmental Risks, Policy Studies Journal, Vol. 28(3), pp. 558-575, doi:10.1111/j.1541-0072.2000.tb02048.x

Heum, Per/Quale, Christian/Karlsen, Jan Erik/ Kragha, Moses/Osahon, George (2003): Enhancement of Local Content in the Upstream Oil and Gas Industry in Nigeria. Institute for Research in Economics and Business Administration, Bergen. Accessible under: https://brage.bibsys.no/xmlui/handle /11250/164539 (10.29.2017).

ILAIPP (Latin American Network for Public Policy Research) (2016): Latin American Initiative for Public Policy Research. Accessible under: http://ilaipp.org/ (10.19.2017).

International Crisis Group (2007): Ecuador. Superando la Inestabilidad, International Crisis Group, Bogota.

Keck, Margaret/Sikkink, Kathryn (1999): Transnational advocacy networks in international and regional politics, International Social Science Journal, Vol. 51(159), pp. 89/101.

Lázaro Rüther, Lena/Müller, Ulrich/Peláez Jara, Melani (2014): Cooperation with Global Networks, in: Lázaro Rüther, Lena/Ayala Martínez, Citlali/Müller, Ulrich (eds.): Global Funds and Networks. Narrowing the Gap between Global Policies and National Implementation, Nomos, Baden-Baden, pp. 127-155.

Mendizabal, Enrique (2010): On the business model and how this affects what think tanks do. Accessible under: https://onthinktanks.org/articles/on-the-business-model-and-how-this-affects-what-think-tanks-do/ (10.19.2017).

Morales, Marcela/Herrera, Juan José/Jarrín, Sebastián (2016): Local Content Frameworks in Latin American Oil and Gas Sectors. Lessons from Ecuador and Colombia, Practical Action, Peru.

Ortiz, Christian (2012): La Sociedad Civil Ecuatoriana en el Laberinto de la Revolución Ciudadana, FLACSO, Quito. Accesible under: http://repositorio.flacsoandes.edu.ec /bitstream/10469/5702/2/TFLACSO-2012CAOL.pdf (29.10.2017).

Recalde, Eulalia (2014): Análisis de las principales transformaciones del Estado Ecuatoriano 2007-2012, Senplades, Quito.

RLIE (Red Latinoamericana sobre las Industrias Extracticas) (2016): Latin American Network on Extractive Industries. Accessible under: http://www.redextractivas.org/ index.php?option=com_content&view=article&id=75&Itemid=570&lang=es (10.19.2017).

Stone, Diane (2001): Think Tanks. Global Lesson-Drawing and Networking Social Policy Ideas, Global Social Policy, Vol. 1(3), pp. 338-360.

Stone, Diane (2002): Introduction. Global knowledge and advocacy networks, Global Networks, Vol. 2(1), pp. 1-12, doi:10.1111/1471-0374.00023

Stone, Diane (2008): Global Public Policy, Transnational Policy Communities, and Their Networks, The Policy Studies Journal, Vol. 36(1), pp. 19/38.

Tordo, Silvana/Anouti, Yahya (2013): Local Content in the Oil and Gas Sector. Case Studies, World Bank, Washington.

United Nations General Assembly (2015): Transforming Our World. The 2030 Agenda for Sustainable Development. Accessible under: http://www.un.org/ga/search/view_ doc.asp?symbol=A/RES/70/1&Lang=E (10.19.2017).

A Dialogue of Knowledge Systems between Indigenous Farmers, Extension Agents and Researchers: Experiences in Bolivia, Colombia and Mexico

Horacio Rodríguez Vázquez

Introduction

The process of Knowledge Sharing, or knowledge exchange, is closely linked to innovation. In fact, innovation happens when changes occur that improve a particular process starting with the generation, exchange and, above all, application of knowledge, technology and information.

In the case of the rural sector in general, and agricultural activities in particular, the flow of information, technology and knowledge from research centres and academic institutions toward landholders saw an upswing toward the end of the nineteenth century, when the notion of rural extension emerged in the United States of America. Later, starting in the 1950s, the concept of agricultural extension spread to Latin America and the Caribbean, and gained momentum with the Green Revolution, which was promoted in Mexico by Norman Borlaug.

Since then, the idea of agricultural extension has evolved from a top-down, linear transfer of technology – from a researcher (the possessor of knowledge) to a producer (the passive recipient of the knowledge) through the support of an extension agent (the intermediary) – toward formats with a broader perspective, based on innovation systems or networks. There, producers' ancestral wisdom is recognized and innovation is fostered through a genuine flow of knowledge in multiple directions among the actors in the agro-food chain (from producer to producer, from researcher to producer, from producer to researcher, from producer to extension agent, from extension agent to wholesaler, etc.).

When working with indigenous populations, the knowledge exchange takes on a particular tone, which is influenced by a number of factors, ranging from language barriers to world view, belief system and local culture, including self-management processes and decision-making within a particular community.

In this regard, the aim of this chapter is to highlight the importance of Knowledge Sharing for agricultural innovation in indigenous communities, based on a dialogue of knowledge systems between producers, rural extension service providers and researchers in Latin America. For this purpose, three experiences will be analysed, supported by international cooperation in Bolivia, Colombia and Mexico: PachaGrama, the Agro-Climate Technical Forums (MTAs) and the experience of Toojil Xíimbal for promoting sustainability in Mayan milpas, respectively.

The text is divided into four parts, not including this introduction. In the first part, the role of Knowledge Sharing in agricultural innovation systems will be discussed, highlighting the importance of rural extension programs. Next is a brief description of international cooperation experiences in the area of Knowledge Sharing with indigenous communities in the selected countries, emphasizing participation by indigenous producers who have shared their knowledge. Based on these experiences, the third section draws on the main lessons learned, in the hopes that they may serve as a departure point for future experiences in Knowledge Sharing with indigenous communities. Finally, the conclusions focus on the importance of enabling knowledge exchange and capacities development as means to foster innovation in rural indigenous communities. Furthermore, the process of Knowledge Sharing will be linked to indigenous communities and key tools for international cooperation, such as the Nagoya Protocol.

The dialogue of knowledge systems and their role in agricultural innovation

Agricultural innovation requires close coordination and collaboration between producers, suppliers, extension agents, public authorities and institutions (both national and sub-national), businesses, the academia and civil society, organized to enable the flow of information and knowledge to build innovation capacities at each of the links in the agro-food chain.

Along these lines, Simón Parisca[1] indicates that the old paradigm of innovation – where innovation is only considered to be the result of scientific research and technological development – ignores many people who may not fall under the traditional profile of "innovator," including all those who have no advanced knowledge and/or higher education in specialized scientific/technological areas. According to the author, innovation should no longer be considered the work of a "creative" few – but rather become a collective act, and the responsibility of all.

---

1   Parisca 2010.

In the rural sector, extension programs represent an essential element in agricultural innovation[2]. Traditionally, research and extension work are developed according to linear, unidirectional models oriented toward increasing agricultural productivity (crop outputs): information and knowledge were generated in research centres and/or academic institutions; then extension agents were trained in the knowledge and, through them, the knowledge and technology developed was able to reach producers – without spaces or processes to allow for feedback.

However, since the 1970s a range of different initiatives have advocated for incorporating producers and their knowledge by way of a number of different rural extension methodologies, such as on-farm research. Thus, both producers and extension agents were trained on agricultural plots by way of a system of calls at key moments for the crops; or participatory research, where the research obtains information from the producer regarding management issues using a survey-style methodology, but with a nonetheless vertical or top-down approach. In recent decades, rural extension services have been operated based on innovation networks, supported by strategic and adaptive research with a territorial approach – where the extension agent is seen as an advisor on innovation and the producer and his or her knowledge as the focus of the intervention[3].

As such, rather than just a static concept, extension work is seen nowadays as a dynamic process involving multiple actors, sectors and dimensions, the principles of which can adopt different methods and/or strategies depending on the territory's political, socioeconomic and agro-ecological environment, as well as the profiles of actors involved. Its aim is to improve the quality of life of producers by way of systematic support – the generation, adaptation and appropriation of technologies and sustainable agricultural management systems, as well as the creation, strengthening and anchoring of the capacities of actors involved in the agricultural innovation system[4].

As can be observed in Figure 1, the current vision of rural extension programs is based around five main pillars or axes, which are interrelated and overlap among themselves: 1) technical support; 2) technological transfer; 3) capacity development; 4) social inclusion; and 5) communication for development and innovation. These pillars are supported by research, technological development and innovation (R+D+i) and must be oriented towards

---

2   Muñoz/Santoyo 2010.
3   Rodríguez 2015a.
4   Rodríguez 2015b.

the market and value chains, as well as being equipped with tools to provide the information and communications technology for agriculture (ICT4Ag).

Figure 1: Components of rural extension programs within the framework of agricultural innovation

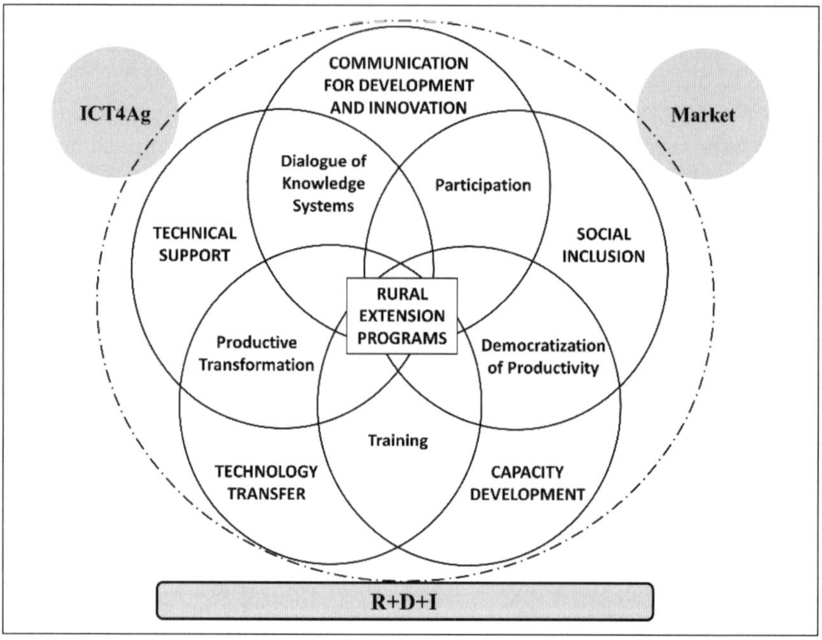

Source: Created by the author.

The above conceptualisation gives a primary role to development communication processes in general, and to participation and dialogues of knowledge systems in particular, aimed at promoting an exchange of knowledge to favour processes of agricultural innovation in the rural sector. In other words, contemporary extension programs must facilitate the process of Knowledge Sharing between different actors along the agro-food chain in order to be effective.

In an interview, Álvaro Urrieta, a cactus producer from the community of Tlalnepantla, Morelos (Mexico) and member of the Mexican Network for Family, Smallholder and Indigenous Agriculture:

> "Extension programs should be closely linked to the wisdom of rural communities, historically determined by their ancestral practices, which hold information associated with decades and centuries of ties with the land as a source of food. This wis-

dom must also, at the same time, be incorporated into new cognitive dynamics derived from advancements made by agricultural science, in a way that strengthens what has been built over time, based on feedback with scientific and technological development linked to agriculture ..."[5]

Based on this framework, the following section presents three case studies of rural extension programs fuelled by international cooperation in Bolivia, Colombia and México, where the process of knowledge exchange with indigenous communities has been a fundamental part of carrying out interventions.

Experiences of international cooperation in Knowledge Sharing with Latin American indigenous communities

PachaGrama (Plurinational State of Bolivia)

PachaGrama is a tool to support Agro-Climate management processes, based on ancient systems of observation and prediction and their natural indicators, such as the movements of stars, animal behaviour and the flowering of plants, among others. This instrument enables qualitative recording of the daily fluctuations in climate and of the main meteorological events associated with a particular crop (rains, lunar cycles, frosts, etc.), using simple icons to identify the different phenomena and their intensity.

It was designed by indigenous Yapuchiris[6] in collaboration with the Association for the Promotion of Sustainability and Shared Knowledge

---

5   Personal statement by Álvaro Urrieta Fernández, Presidente de la Unión de Productores e Introductores de Hortalizas de la Central de Abastos de la Ciudad de México, in an interview on June 30, 2015.

6   *Yapuchiri* is an Aymara word meaning agricultural producer. It emerged in 2004 out of a producers' initiative known as the "seed" group, which took on the task of critically analysing the characteristics of agricultural production and communicating their experiences and knowledge to other producers. In other words, they were managing innovation and the adoption of technology to support agricultural production. The concept of the Yapuchiri is associated with the development of leadership abilities in the management of the productive system, using processes of innovation and constant experimentation in tandem with ancient wisdom. Yapuchiris adapt practices, experiences and knowledge to their local conditions. The management of their plots and the results obtained, whether successes or failures – support their role as producers who mobilize knowledge and productive action (Ricaldi/Aguilar 2014).

117

(PROSUCO) within the framework of the Disaster Risk Reduction Program; Phase III (2010-2014) of the Swiss Agency for Development and Cooperation (COSUDE); it was then made available to the Vice Minister of Rural and Agricultural Development (VDRA) of the Ministry for Rural and Land Development (MDRyT) of the Plurinational State of Bolivia for scaling up using an extension strategy. This strategy is based on the formation of leaders and participation processes within an intercultural framework, conducting research on ancient Agro-Climate knowledge systems and giving recognition to their value.

This record has enabled extension agents and producers to systematize ancestral knowledge to give short, medium and long-term explanations of climate phenomena on a local level, the identification of atypical climate patterns over the agricultural cycle, thresholds for damages to crops in order to design and/or activate early-warning systems, as well as information on good practices in facing the challenges implied by these phenomena. As such, PachaGrama is useful to producers, researchers and decision-makers in the process of exchanging technical information, practices, knowledge and strategies, enabling agricultural capital (land, supplies, seeds, labour, etc.) to be used in the most appropriate way, in the best possible time and place for managing the risk of productive losses in the context of climate change. PachaGrama has even been useful in defining new lines of research and innovation needs in the area of Climate-Smart Agriculture[7].

Currently, PachaGrama is an initiative of MDRyT with funding from the COSUDE, and technical and operating support provided by HELVETAS Swiss Intercooperation, PROSUCO, the Andean Community of Nations (CAN) and the German Agency for International Cooperation (GIZ).

Agro-Climate Technical Forums (Colombia)

Within the framework of the Program for Research on Climate Change, Agriculture and Food Security (CCAFS) of the Consultative Group for International Agricultural Research (CGIAR), the International Centre for Tropical Agriculture (CIAT) has established Agro-Climate Technical Forums (MTAs) in the Colombian departments of Córdoba, Sucre and Cauca. The MTAs seek to bring together key actors from the local agricultural sector to provide information, especially to smallholders, on the changes in climate expected in their region, as they may affect their crops and the kinds of

---

7   FIDA 2013.

strategies that can be implemented to keep negative outcomes to a minimum.

MTAs are spaces for discussion between different public and private actors such as the Ministry of Agriculture and Rural Development in Colombia (MADR), departmental Ministries of Agriculture, Farmers' Associations, Autonomous Regional Corporations (CARs), universities, producers' associations, Municipal Technical Assistance Units (UMATAs) and research centres, among others. Their aim is to manage local Agro-Climate information in order to integrate knowledge and best practices in adaptation to climate phenomena, which are then shared with technical experts and local producers using a document called the regional Agro-Climate Bulletin[8].

In deference to this chapter's common thread, a special emphasis is given to the MTA of Cauca, established in November of 2014, and comprising a membership of mainly smallholders from indigenous communities in the Polindara, Coconuco, Puracé and Quintana sectors. Due to the profile of the farmers involved, CCAFS's systems and Agro-Climate models were adapted to use climate indicators that have been used by indigenous communities since ancient times, enabling improvements to Agro-Climate predictions and analyses using pre-Columbian knowledge and direct participation by producers in data gathering. As a result of these interactions and the exchange between community and scientific knowledge, as of December of 2015 Cauca's MTA had generated ten Agro-Climate Bulletins on the local effects of the climate on mainly corn, potato, bean, pea and onion crops, including recommendations on best practices, by and for producers, with the aim of minimizing adverse climate impacts on their output.

The Cauca MTA is the result of an alliance established between the Fundación Procuenca Río Piedras, Empresa de Acueducto de Popayán and the rural communities involved, and currently benefits from the technical and financial support of MADR, CCAFS-CGIAR, GIZ and the Colombian Institute of Meteorology, Hydrology and Environmental Studies (IDEAM).

Sustainable Mayan Milpas – Toojil Xíimbal (Mexico)

Toojil Xíimbal ("justice on the move") is a Mayan indigenous organisation that was legally incorporated as a cooperative in 2011. Its focus is on

---

8   CCAFS 2015.

strengthening identity based on native seeds and the traditional cultivation system known as the Mayan milpa[9].

With the technical support of The Nature Conservancy (TNC) and funding from the United States Agency for International Development (USAID) within the framework of the Alianza México REDD+[10]. In late 2013 and early 2014, Toojil Xíimbal initiated a project for sustainable Mayan milpas in the municipality of Hopelchén, Campeche, incorporating new conservation practices with indigenous knowledge, such as obtaining a sedentary instead of itinerant milpa, eliminating burning off and incorporating organic compost. In this way, the use of local native seeds is recovered, and the Mayan milpa productive system is made more efficient based on certain specific improvements in agricultural management practices affecting the fertility and conservation of soils.

In Knowledge Sharing, this initiative addresses the conservation and exchange of native seeds from farmer to farmer, as well as providing workshops and participatory processes for reviewing, according to the members of the Mayan cooperative, "what is most useful from both worlds – what we learned from our grandparents, and today's innovations that make more sustainable agriculture possible"[11]. Similarly, the project aims to establish a farmers' school in the community of Suctuc, on the outskirts of Hopelchén, an initiative expected to be achieved within ten years.

---

9   The word *milpa* is a generic term referring to the agricultural and cultural system used by a range of Mesoamerican indigenous ethnic groups in the cultivation of local varieties of maize and a number of other agricultural species. It comes from the náhuatl word *milli*, a planted lot, and *pan*, on top of, meaning literally "what is planted on top of a lot." There are a range of *milpa* systems currently in use in Mexico, each one adapted by a pre-Hispanic culture according to climate conditions, slope and region. The Mayan *milpa* is an agro-forestry and cultural system that is still used by Mayan groups from the rainforests of the Yucatán Peninsula to cultivate native species of maize, beans and squash. Also, throughout the course of the agricultural cycle these groups carry out a set of rituals which offer a view to their way of seeing the world, in which they ask permission and give thanks to the forest deities (Rodríguez et al. 2016).

10 The Alianza México REDD+ is an initiative by a number of civil society organisations (The Nature Conservancy, Rainforest Alliance, Espacios Naturales y Desarrollo Sustentable and Woods Hole Research Center) in collaboration with the aim of supporting the Mexican government in preparing for REDD+. It receives funding from USAID in the framework of the project AID-523-A-II-0000I (Proyecto de Reducción de Emisiones por la Deforestación y la Degradación de Bosques de México).

11 Cepeda/Amoroso 2016.

Based on these experiences, Table 1 shows an attempted systematisation to highlight the modalities of Knowledge Sharing being applied. While each case has different beneficiaries, all three show that the process of Knowledge Sharing is fostered based on dialogue and the exchange of information, best practices, technology and knowledge mainly among the leaders of indigenous communities and researchers. Furthermore, this exchange is enhanced by the central role played by civil society organisations as local facilitators of the process.

Table 1. Systematisation of international cooperation experiences in Knowledge Sharing with indigenous communities in Bolivia, Colombia and Mexico.

Initiative (Country)	Donor partner(s)	Recipient partner	Knowledge Sharing outline
PachaGrama (Bolivia)	*Financial cooperation:* • COSUDE *Technical cooperation:* • HELVETAS Swiss Intercooperation • PROSUCO • CAN • GIZ	• MDRyT (national government)	• Enhancement of ancient observation systems and their natural indicators on Agro-Climate information on a local level.
MTA Cauca (Colombia)	*Financial cooperation:* • CCAFS/CGIAR *Technical cooperation:* • CIAT	• Fundación Procuenca Río Piedras (Local Civil Society Organisation (CSO)).	• Dialogue fora between researchers and indigenous producers to generate recommendations on best agricultural practices in the context of climate change.
Sustainable Mayan *Milpa*, Hopelchén (Mexico)	• USAID • TNC	• Toojil Xíimbal (indigenous cooperative)	• Participatory workshops to fuse ancient production knowledge with new technological innovations.

Source: Created by the author.

121

Lessons learned on Knowledge Sharing in indigenous communities

Knowledge Sharing events with indigenous communities must give special relevance to the context and to local actors, promoting a territorial approach from a broader perspective, considering the physical, climate and agro-ecological characteristics of the territory, as well as ancestral wisdom, worldview, culture and interactions between different actors (both public and private) within the local productive system. For this to occur, these activities must be designed, planned and executed with a high level of participation, as well as promoting channels for constant feedback. As observed in Table 1 of the previous section, participation by local partners who know the local reality, such as community organisations, agricultural community leaders/innovators and/or promotors, is key to the process of rural extension and innovation.

When working with indigenous communities, extension programs must emphasize the creation of integral improvements in the quality of life of producers and their families, taking into account their world view and the different aspects of life in the community and the rural setting, rather than centering their efforts exclusively on increasing crop outputs. As such, the extension method used with this sector of the population is very important. Long term participatory processes, as well as farmer-to-farmer methodologies supported by training strategies that use simple, practical, everyday language – preferably in the farmers' native language – and which highlight the importance of rural youth and women, have shown themselves to be more effective in improving the impact and ensuring the sustainability of extension programs with rural indigenous groups[12].

The above requires staff that are trained in andragogy, but who also understand local realities and are sensitized to the culture, ways and customs of the community. This is the basis of the importance of identifying the leading producers (in terms of innovation, rather than the political context) and fostering the incorporation of promoters from a specific indigenous community, or who at least live there and know the local language and culture. Furthermore, and of particular interest to Knowledge Sharing processes in academic institutions, it is essential to review the training processes of future extension agents (agronomists, sociologists, veterinarians, anthropologies, etc.) in universities, taking into account the development of technical competencies while not neglecting social capacities and abilities

---

12   Rodríguez 2015b.

which enable innovation, entrepreneurship and intercultural exchanges, especially for the purposes of managing and resolving conflicts. This does not imply the development of "know-it-all" extension agents, but rather technical professionals with the ability to work as part of multidisciplinary teams.

On the other hand, the experiences analysed show that research and extension work must be designed and carried out according to demand, adapted to the local context and the needs of producers and their plots. This allows the producer, extension agents and researchers to choose the most effective and efficient combination of practices and technology for a particular community, region or unit of production. Finally, the process of Knowledge Sharing with indigenous producers should consider systematic, timely interventions in terms of training, technology transfer, technical support, communication and outreach. In this respect, rural colleges and community centres play a central role. Similarly, it is very important to generate and seek out synergies with other institutions and organisations in order to extend communication to large-scale channels, such as television and community radio.

In recent years, aspects related to rights to traditional knowledge have been incorporated into different interventions and the overall debate on Knowledge Sharing processes with indigenous communities. The interest of large multinationals in genetic resources and patenting them for their own exclusive use, especially in the agricultural, pharmaceutical and food industries, puts at risk certain faculties of first peoples regarding the use and exploitation of certain genetic resources, especially in indigenous communities. One of the measures taken to address this issue is the The Nagoya Protocol on Access to Genetic Resources and the Fair and Equitable Sharing of Benefits Arising from their Utilisation to the Convention on Biological Diversity, adopted on October 29, 2010 at the tenth Conference of the Parties (COP10) held in Japan. The Nagoya Protocol took effect in October of 2014, with a current total of 69 signatory countries.

Accordingly, one international development cooperation project in support of the implementation of the Nagoya protocol is currently underway between the Mexican Government's National Commission for Biodiversity Study and Use (CONABIO) and the Federal Ministry of Economic Cooperation and Development (BMZ) from German. The project is called "Fair and equitable participation and the benefits to be obtained from the use and management of biological diversity;" it started in 2013 and is expected to run until 2017, and its aim is to promote the enforcement of regulations and guidelines for access to genetic resources and traditional wisdom, and to ensure a fair and equitable participation in the benefits obtained from their utilisation, thereby creating incentives for protection and sustainable use of biological diversity.

Conclusions

The process of Knowledge Sharing with indigenous communities should be focused on ensuring the creation, development and strengthening of local capacities, in order to enable ownership, shared responsibility and sustainability in innovation over time. As such, it is important to acknowledge and promote the agency of producers, recognising them as active agents for change, rather than as passive recipients of external aid (agents vs. patients). In other words, instead of a transfer of knowledge, information and/or technology, the process should involve facilitation of knowledge exchange and innovation-oriented capacity development in all actors with ties to the local productive system (suppliers, producers, community leaders, researchers, extension agents, traders, etc.).

In a broader sense, agricultural innovation initiatives (be they local, regional or national) must promote a portfolio of tools that foster Knowledge Sharing by building and strengthening networks of learning, as well as the creation of public-private partnerships focused on research, development and innovation (R+D+i). However, it is important to remember that these innovations do not exclusively involve products or processes in the local productive system, but rather must mainly be concerned with social and human capital, the organic structure of the local public administration, articulation with the academia and cooperation networks among adjoining communities and territories, both urban and rural.

One aspect that appears obvious, but which is nonetheless often neglected, is that, however much training and technology transfer and however many workshops and other activities are tied to agricultural innovation and extension systems, final decisions are in the hands of producers, based on their belief systems and the resources (financial, technical and human) available to them – an aspect that is further exposed by cultural factors when working with indigenous groups. For this reason, when designing a Knowledge Sharing intervention strategy in the rural sector, it is very important that producers formulate their own approach on the original problem to solve, be permanent participants during the process and finally, take strategic decisions that undertake their ancestral knowledge adapting it to technology aligned to their cultural standards and vision of development.

Bibliography

CCAFS (Program for Research on Climate Change, Agriculture and Food Security) (2015): Acercando los pronósticos estacionales a las necesidades de los agricultores, CGIAR, Cali.

Cepeda, Carolina/Amoroso, Ariel (2016): Experiencias de desarrollo rural sustentable y conservación en la Península de Yucatán, The Nature Conservancy, México.

FIDA (Fondo Internacional de Desarrollo Agrícola) (2013): Programa de Inclusión Económica para Familias y Comunidades Rurales en el Territorio del Estado Plurinacional de Bolivia (ACCESOS) con financiación proveniente del Programa de Adaptación para la Agricultura de Pequeña Escala (ASAP). Informe final sobre el diseño del Programa, FIDA, FIDA, Rome.

Muñoz Rodríguez, Manrrubio/Santoyo Cortés, Vinicio Horacio (2010): Del extensionismo a las redes de innovación, in: Aguilar Ávila, Jorge/Altamirano Cárdenas, Javier Reyes/Rendón Medel, Roberto (eds.): Del extensionismo agrícola a las redes de innovación rural, Chapingo, México, pp. 31-69.

Parisca, Simón Antonio (2010): ¿Gerencia de la innovación o innovación en la gerencia...?, in: Leone, Antonio (ed.): PYMES. Factor de integración. 35 años de esfuerzo continuo del SELA, Editorial Horizonte, Lima, pp. 79-90.

Ricaldi Arévalo, Tania/Aguilar, Luis Carlos (2014): Los yapuchiris. Capacidades locales en la gestión del riesgo climático, LEISA Revista de Agroecología, Vol. 30(3), Asociación Ecología, Tecnología y Cultura en los Andes en convenio con la Fundación ILEIA, Perú, pp. 26-27.

Rodríguez Canto, Adolfo/González Moctezuma, Pablo/Flores Torres, Jorge/Nava Montero, Rutilio/Dzib Aguilar, Luis Antonio/Pérez Pérez, Juan Ramón/Thüerbeck, Nadja/González Iturbe, José Antonio (2016): Milpas de las comunidades mayas y dinámica de uso de suelo en la Península de Yucatán, Alianza México REDD+, México.

Rodríguez Vázquez, Horacio (2015a): El aporte de los centros de investigación a los sistemas nacionales de extensión rural. Experiencias del CIMMYT en México, Presentation at the I Congreso Boliviano de Asistencia Técnica y Extensiòn Rural on the 12th of November at the Instituto Nacional de Innovación Agropecuaria y Forestal, Ministerio de Desarrollo Rural y Tierras, La Paz.

Rodríguez Vázquez, Horacio (2015b): Extensionismo y agricultura familiar: Recomendaciones para una estrategia integral. EnlACe: La revista de la Agricultura de Conservación. 24 de febrero/22-24 de marzo, SAGARPA, CIMYYT, México.

Knowledge Sharing as a Way of Life, or a Means of Survival

José Iván Égido Zurita

"My acts are more mine when they are as well the acts of everybody"[1]

Indigenous peoples' persistence in "continuing to be" does not consist, in most cases, of remaining static or of taking purely defensive positions in the face of permanent changes and encounters, but rather the opposite. One of the most obvious of many paradoxes concerning human cultures is this: as humans, we find meaning or coherence in our lives by looking at others, rather than by looking directly at ourselves[2]. The way in which such a view can reassure, discomfort or frighten lastly points to the kind of relationship that has been established between individuals and groups of individuals.

Of course, these relationships are not necessarily harmless or peaceful – on the contrary, they are determined by each person or group's unequal access to material resources, knowledge and ties to others. One clear example of such unequal access is the precarious or non-existent inclusion of indigenous peoples into the economic and political structure in many countries – as well as the exploitation they suffer at the hands of other groups and people[3]. The learning, exchange and negotiation of knowledge are practices that exist across human cultures. Indigenous cultures are no exception. In fact, in recent years these practices have led to significant exchanges between different indigenous groups, and with non-indigenous populations.

---

1   Octavio Paz; translated by the author from Spanish to English. The line cited in the Spanish original is: "los actos míos son más míos si son también de todos" (Paz 1989: 98).
2   In this respect, many authors have made reference to this understanding of "what is human", including biologists Gregory Bateson (1972), Humberto Maturana (Maturana 1997: 144), and others, who have developed new perspectives on understanding learning and culture. These trends were the basis for new disciplines such as cybernetics, in the case of Bateson, or the systemic focus or autopoiesis, later applied in sociology by Niklas Luhmann, in the case of Maturana. Also of use here are reflections by Roger Bartra on "consciousness" (Bartra 2014: 300).
3   See: United Nations DESA 2009; World Bank 2015; among others.

The focus of this chapter is on describing exchanges between indigenous peoples, as well as strategies they have employed in the process of exchanging and sharing their knowledge and experiences in the political field, specifically while working toward obtaining recognition of their collective rights during the process of drafting the Bolivian constitution of 2009. For example, the ways in which perspectives on "the other" came into play in the application of these strategies will be described, showing a transition from knowledge transfer to Knowledge Sharing.

This chapter is structured in three parts: the first will address the conceptual approach of Knowledge Sharing; the second will describe the historical context of the Constituent Assembly of Bolivia; finally, the third part will conclude by describing the process of articulation and alliance-building to optimize participation by indigenous peoples in the Constituent Assembly in what has become known as the "Unity Pact of the Constituent Assembly."

Indigenous knowledge and Knowledge Sharing

Over the last few decades, a number of multilateral and bilateral institutions[4] together with organisations representing indigenous peoples have embarked on a process of revival, recovery and protection of indigenous knowledge. Since the beginning of the 1950s, anthropologists and ethnologists – many of them self-identified ethno-scientists – have been researching and developing the subject of *indigenous knowledge*[5]. Not only did they initiate debate on diversity and differences between mutually-interrelated branches of knowledge, they also developed concepts such as indigenous intellectual property, as well as compensation and protection of the same within the context of trans- and intercultural interaction[6].

The subject of *indigenous knowledge* developed much more quickly once it was in the hands of international multilateral organisations. In fact, the agencies and organisations of the United Nations lent their support by way

---

4   Foremost among them are the United Nations Educational, Scientific and Cultural Organisation (UNESCO) and Food and Agriculture Organisation (FAO). The *International Social Science Journal* dedicated an entire issue to indigenous knowledge (Agrawal 2002; UNESCO 2002; Leach/Fairhead 2002).

5   Conklin 1957, Lewis 1975 and Wyman 1964 as cited in Agrawal 2002: 287.

6   Agrawal 2002: 287.

of a number of Conventions[7], Declarations[8] and Resolutions[9]. These international documents bring into sharp relief the use and distribution of indigenous knowledge in protecting the environment (for instance, as a defense mechanism against climate change) and as part of management of natural resources[10]. As such, indigenous knowledge is emerging as a new and influential contribution to global scientific policy[11].

Indigenous Knowledge, according to the definition proposed by UNESCO-CIRAN[12] (United Nations Educational, Scientific and Cultural Organisation - Centre for International Research and Advisory Networks), refers to traditional or local knowledge with roots in a community that is unique to that particular culture, place or society[13]. In other words, the concept refers to knowledge and competencies that fall outside the formal education system and that allow the community to survive. Such knowledge is dynamic and is the result of continuous processes of experimentation, innovation and adaptation[14].

---

7   The preamble to UNESCO's Convention on the Protection and Promotion of the Diversity of Cultural Expressions recognizes "the importance of traditional knowledge as a source of intangible and material wealth, and in particular the knowledge systems of indigenous peoples, and its positive contribution to sustainable development, as well as the need for its adequate protection and promotion" (UNESCO 2005).

8   On the contribution of indigenous knowledge, see UNESCO 2001, Annex II, Paragraph 14.
    On the right of indigenous peoples to maintain, control, protect and develop their knowledge, see UN Declaration on the Rights of Indigenous Peoples 2007 (UN 2007).

9   The Sendai Framework for Disaster Risk Reduction 2015-2030, outcome of the Third UN World Conference on Disaster Risk Reduction held in Sendai (Japan) from March 14-18, 2015, acknowledges the need for broader diffusion of indigenous and local knowledge on preventing natural disasters and recognizes its contribution to the development of plans and mechanisms for natural disaster risk management (SAB-UNGA 2016: 11, Paragraph 36, Part V).

10 See also chapter 5 in this volume by Horacio Rodríguez.

11 The Intergovernmental Panel on Climate Change (IPCC), concludes in its 2014 report on climate change that indigenous, local and traditional knowledge systems constitute an essential resource for adapting to climate change, and that integrating these knowledge systems into existing adaptation practices will render them more effective (UNESCO 2015: 15).

12 UNESCO-CIRAN 2003.

13 Grenier 1998, in: UNESCO-CIRAN 2003.

14 UNESCO-CIRAN 2003.

In this context, indigenous and local knowledge is being recovered, its value recognized, and is even being equated with the knowledge produced by Western or modern science[15]. On the other hand, while the positioning of different indigenous knowledge systems in relation to dominant knowledge systems is by no means innocuous or free of controversy in the academic and political spheres[16], the diversity of indigenous peoples also frames a diversity of indigenous knowledge systems which are interlinked, in a way that is at times complementary, at other times fraught with tension.

In this context, finding a connection between the different indigenous knowledge systems also constitutes a challenge, as this endeavour departs from a relationship that is characterized by the mere transmission and/or imposition of knowledge to one based on knowledge exchange and/or Knowledge Sharing.

Knowledge Sharing is defined as the process by which a person or group of people make knowledge available to others, both consciously and willingly, without any implication of having surrendered ownership of said knowledge; rather, the result is joint ownership between the original owners of the knowledge and those with whom the knowledge is shared[17]. As such, this process can be divided into two sub-processes: externalisation (whereby an individual surrenders knowledge to others) and internalisation (whereby the recipient finds meaning in the knowledge received). In other words, Knowledge Sharing requires two actions to occur at the same time: giving and receiving, also requiring the individual to be able to "combine ideas, visions, and information that were previously unrelated, enabling the construction of new knowledge based on that which is possessed by others"[18].

Ulrich Müller in his chapter on competences for Knowledge Sharing proposes a series of conditions for generating factors conducive to successful

---

15   In its report from October 2016, the Scientific Advisory Board of the United Nations General Assembly (SAB-UNGA) affirmed that it had taken a number of different decisions considering indigenous and local knowledge to be both complementary and integral to scientific knowledge (SAB-UNGA 2016).

16   Effectively, debates on indigenous knowledge have been shifted by an emphasis on conceptual and moral discord; and autonomy among knowledge systems confronted with the emphasis on the modern system, or urban science, which is supported by science and knowledge as produced by institutions and "experts" (Leach/Fairhead 2002: 299).

17   Ipe 2003 as cited in: Camelo et al. 2010: 116.

18   Camelo et al. 2010: 116.

Knowledge Sharing[19]. Among them are the following conditions related to the quality of communication and competencies on each side with regard to: i) *self-reflection:* All sides are committed, open and ready to teach and learn; ii) *a common reflection on a problem:* a joint perspective on the issue to which Knowledge Sharing is to be applied; iii) *reflection on communication and cooperation between parties:* trusting relationships and a common language between parties; and iv) *methods of reflection:* appropriate formats and facilitation for placing and contextualizing the process of joint creation, and openness to innovation by those involved. Another condition that enables Knowledge Sharing is a social and cultural context characterized by societies open to external influence, which have a clear national identity, respect freedom of opinion and minority voices[20].

This conceptual framework sets out the description of the Knowledge Sharing process between indigenous peoples in Bolivia, during the aforementioned process of drafting the Bolivian constitution during the first decade of the twenty-first century.

Indigenous peoples and the Constituent Assembly

Political processes in all regions have their precedents in another region. Particularly in Latin America, this appears to be something of a rule. As such, just as the turmoil in Napoleonic Spain gave way to the first cries for independence in the Americas at the beginning of the nineteenth century[21], the currents of constitutional law first in Spain and/or Europe, then the United States, also influenced a number of Latin American legal institutions.[22]

Nonetheless, from the point of view of indigenous peoples, the Law from both the Colonial and post-Independence periods represented only a law formally in force but not a living law related with their experiences and convictions[23].

In effect, the "constitutionalism" of the nineteenth and twentieth centuries tended to define the Constitution as a rigid document with a focus on

---

19   See chapter 2 in this volume by Ulrich Müller.
20   See chapter 2 in this volume by Ulrich Müller.
21   See: Luna de Sola (1978); Bethell (1991): 280.
22   Gros 2002: 147.
23   Ibid.: 144.

institutional organisation, which also gave symbolic value to an ideal, rather than as a regulatory text based in reality. In other words, it was an expression of a modern civilisation opposed to rural barbarism. The reality of this constitutionalism ran parallel to legal regulation[24], to such an extent that during the nineteenth and twentieth century peaceful, uninterrupted constitutional continuity was not to be seen[25]. Neither did the constitutions of the time make any significant reference to indigenous populations and their collective rights. This omission was justified using the flimsy excuse of a deceptive understanding of the principle of equality before the law, which translated into real discrimination and political, social and economic exclusion[26].

From a purely political perspective, the Mexican and Russian Revolutions led in 1917 to the emergence of a new approach by the Latin American left that foreshadowed a new tendency in attention to indigenous peoples' issues, exemplified by Mareátegui, founder of the Communist Party of Peru, followed by the Communist Party of Ecuador, which later created the Ecuadorian Federation of Indians. Decades later in Bolivia, and inspired by its predecessor in Mexico, the 1952 Revolution led to recognition of indigenous citizenship and basic social rights under a "civilizing" vision that reduced indigenous people to "peasants" ("*campesino*" in Spanish)[27].

In this context, the Andean region saw in an era of constitutional reforms during the 1990s, which gave recognition to the multicultural nature of these societies (Peru in 1993 and Bolivia in 1994). Ecuador went further still in 1998 with its new constitution, by incorporating both intangible property in communal lands and the collective rights of peoples "who define themselves as nations"[28]. Another kind of reform brought in by this new constitutional paradigm is municipal decentralisation, by which greater political participation was to be achieved, significantly increasing the access

---

24   In this way the separation, independence and balance of powers stands in contrast to the predominance of Executive Power that was the legacy of the era of *caudillismo*, military power and government supremacy (Gros 2002: 153).

25   The proliferation of constitutions on the continent in the nineteenth century is significant. The Andean Region is home to the most extreme cases: Peru had eight, Ecuador and Bolivia eleven (Ibid.: 161-162).

26   Ibid.: 147ff.

27   Albó 2008: 232.

28   Ibid.: 245.

of popular organisations, including indigenous organisations, to municipal governments[29].

Conflicts over access to natural resources, identities and names

In the current Bolivian context, over the last forty years, in parallel to constitutional reforms, new indigenous organisations were incorporated, mainly in Lowland regions (that extend from the Amazon Basin in the North to the semiarid Chaco in the South), while older organisations were reconfigured or reincorporated under new names, mainly in the Highlands (Central Plateau – Altiplano - and Interandean Valleys)[30].

This process by which indigenous peoples created organisations, mainly for the Lowland Peoples, was a direct consequence of their need to organize in the face of conflicts arising out of exploitation of the natural resources in their territories by corporations and indigenous groups from other regions known as "colonists"[31].

As such the first Lowlands organisation was founded on the Bolivian plains at the end of the 1970s, in the department of Beni, as a strategy of self-defense in the face of a critical situation of displacement and violence suffered by people from the Mojeño, Yuracaré and Tchimán indigenous groups at the hands of the logging industry. This desperate endeavor in self-defense ended up flowing, ten years later, into the formation of a supra-

---

29   Ibid.: 234ff.
30   Bolivia is divided politically and administratively into nine departments. Of these nine, two are entirely located in the Highlands (Oruro and Potosí); five contain territories that correspond to both the Highlands and the Lowlands (Chuquisaca, Cochabamba, La Paz, Santa Cruz and Tarija) and two (Beni, Pando) are entirely in the Lowlands. The population has historically been concentrated in the highlands, and it is only in the last century that processes of internal colonisation have enabled population and economic growth in the lowland regions.
31   Conflicts between indigenous peoples have occurred and continue to occur, as with most conflict between different stakeholders the world over, concerning access to natural resources and livelihoods. In the case of conflicts between "native" and "colonist" indigenous peoples, these are characterized by access to animal protein (Gómez 1991: 184-185), which was later extended to the use and possession of land for extensive agriculture and livestock farming, which would also deprive indigenous communities of access to their traditional hunting and fishing grounds (Vadillo 2009: 137ff.).

departmental organisation that managed to articulate a strategy for protecting its territories, around the common identity of "indigenous peoples," through the Confederation of Indigenous Peoples of Bolivia.

On the other hand, in the Highlands, the end of the 1980s saw the beginning of a process that sought to recover the cultural identities most specific to the area. This gave rise to the Council of Ayllus and Marqas of Collasuyu (CONAMAQ), which in order to populate its ranks drew from the membership of peasants' organisations that together formed the Single Confederation of Unions of Rural Workers ("campesinos") of Bolivia (CSUTCB) and the "Bartolina Sisa" National Federation of Rural Women ("mujeres campesinas") (FNMC-BS), all of whom identified themselves as "first peoples"[32].

It should be noted that this set of identities constitutes a full deck upon which indigenous peoples can draw as appropriate: the identity or identities to be used can be chosen to suit the particular situation. This happens not only with self-identification, but also with the way in which each person or each organisation sees the others. Therefore, this resource has been highly utilized to qualify or disqualify, such as when CONAMAQ, for instance, sought to consolidate itself by saying that its members were true first peoples, unlike the "peasants" of the CSUTCB[33].

The result was a diverse range of indigenous organisations that described themselves as indigenous, First Peoples, peasants and colonists[34], none of which shared either spaces for coordination or mechanisms for articulation, but rather viewed one another with distrust.

It was in this context that the Constituent Assembly (CA) was established in May of 2006, resulting from five years of continuous social mobilisation

---

32   "Ethnic identity and the status of peasant ("campesinos") are, effectively, two
      different dimensions or perspectives that are in constant interplay – both of them
      with the potential to mobilize – which in many Andean regions coexist within
      the same people and organisations, meaning that in many contexts they can mu-
      tually reinforce one another without necessarily being considered interchangea-
      ble" (Albó 2002: 236). This distinction began, following the Bolivian Revolu-
      tion in 1952, when apart from being granted rights of citizenship such as the
      right to vote and to have private property, indigenous people were stripped of
      recognition of their cultural identity, and instead pigeonholed into the socioeco-
      nomic category of "peasants" ("campesinos").

33   Albó 2002: 236.

34   During the process of drafting the constitution, organisations known as "colo-
      nists", i. e. highland indigenous persons that colonized in the lowlands, at the
      time decided to change their name to "intercultural communities".

characterized by failing governance, with the resignation of two constitutional presidents and premature elections, and demands for autonomy and even independence from a number of departments within Bolivia[35].

The demand for a CA arose from a march that began in the Eastern plains and reached the Central Plateau (around 800 km) in 2002. The march was initiated by indigenous peoples from the Lowlands, and by the time it ended also included participation by CONAMAQ, the indigenous organisation from the Highlands. It should be mentioned that peasants' organisations did not take part, as they were already represented by their own political party (Movimiento al Socialismo, MAS) which decided not to support the mobilisation.

The establishment of the CA in the year 2006 was the work of President Evo Morales, leader of a peasants' organisation representing colonist farmers and representative of the Socialist Movement (MAS), the political party that had been formed by the peasants' organisations.

This brings to light a certain paradox: the return to a belief in the *text* that reflects an ideal for modern society, characteristic of the constitutionalism of the nineteenth and twentieth century, was being promoted by those who had received none of its benefits: indigenous peoples.

Two explanations offer ways to understand this paradox: the first is that following the development of international human rights jurisprudence[36] after the Second World War, indigenous people gained a strategy for penetrating and using the legal and conceptual framework of dominant cultures to obtain mechanisms for protection of their rights[37]. The second explanation refers to the idea that indigenous peoples were influenced by the ties

---

35   See: Valencia/Egido (2010); Garcés (2013), among others.

36   Initiated with the creation of the Study of the Problem of Discrimination against Indigenous Populations; carried out by the Special Rapporteur to the UN Sub-Commission on Prevention of Discrimination and Protection of Minorities, José Martínez Cobo (1971), released in 1985. This report enabled gradual progress toward the approval of a regulatory framework that recognizes and protects the rights of indigenous peoples. This regulatory development was accompanied by the creation of mechanisms for discussion which included, little by little, participation by representatives of indigenous groups. In 1982, the Working Group on Indigenous Populations was created at the heart of the UN Economic and Social Council, which issued recommendations to States and initiated discussion on approving a declaration on protecting the rights of indigenous peoples; the Permanent Forum on Indigenous Issues was created in 1995 (UN 1986).

37   Diego Iturralde (1995) refers to this process as the aggregation of particular and diverse demands of peoples and communities within local and regional spheres,

they have had and continue to have with environmental and human rights organisations, which of course reflect more clearly the "Latin American cultural inclination to overstate the ability of the law to transform reality, or to perceive regulation as a manifestation of a collective symbology or set of images that makes up reality"[38].

The Unity Pact of the Constituent Assembly

The organisations which had spent decades distancing themselves from one another finally found a common aspiration: to achieve a constitutional process that would totally reform the constitution in place at the time. Effectively, in September of 2003, the "Unity Pact of the Constituent Assembly" was created (from here on referred to as simply, "the Pact"), with many of the most representative of the indigenous, peasants' and first peoples' organisations promoting the Convening Act for the process of drafting a new constitution[39]. The actions of the Pact during the first stage (2004 - 2005) was in response to several different conflicts related to proposed laws which threatened to restrict access to natural resources and limit the land rights of indigenous peoples.

After Evo Morales was elected Constitutional President of Bolivia (2005), and the Constituent Assembly was called (2006) the Pact articulated itself again in proposing a document which outlined the textual content of the constitution as proposed by the members of the Constituent Assembly. This document later became the fundamental basis for many of the processes of negotiation, both among members of the Assembly and between political parties.

From this process starting with what was essentially a Constitutional Draft by indigenous peoples, peasants and first peoples (from here on the

---

     followed by the generation of new, unifying categories (such as autonomy, territory and self-determination) and means for symbolisation (such as nation, nationality and indigenous people) that were and are useful for expressing demands and proposing them as part of a global strategy.

38   Casal 2010: 215. Another point of view is reflected by Bolivian philosopher H.C.F. Mansilla: "Faith in the rationality and effectiveness of written texts is very entrenched in Bolivian political culture, despite of numerous experiences over a long period of time showing at best modest practical results for any constitutional changes. Paradoxically, this belief has been and is limited by an also-generalized attitude of fundamental distrust in written law and formal codes" (Mansilla 2014: 99).

39   See: Valencia/Egido (2010); Garcés (2013); among others.

Pact's Proposal), two phenomena in particular should be noted: (1) The different non-governmental organisations working in isolation with many of the Pact's members agreed to work jointly; in other words, they agreed to set aside their institutional rivalries and create an inter-institutional network in support of the Pact; and (2) for the first time, reflections and proposals for sectorial demands were superseded by accords of welfare, not only for the Pact's organisations, but for all Bolivians (there were an idea of "well-being of the public").

The process of creating the Pact Proposal led to a scenario in which a process of Knowledge Sharing was allowed to occur. Indeed, during these meetings the processes of *externalisation* and *internalisation* were in constant interplay, not only with regard to the issues related to the Pact's Proposal but also concerning issues of leadership and mechanisms for funding the work or leaders and managers[40]. There is no doubt that there are many cases of Knowledge Sharing to be found in this process, however the most important one for the purposes of this chapter is to describe how Knowledge Sharing was used to smooth the greatest source of disagreement between the organisations: that of identity.

The shift from self-reflection to a common reflection

Following the European invasion of the Americas, the Colonial Powers lumped indigenous peoples together under generic identities and names such as Indians, *naturales*, etc. Later, the twentieth century brought in processes by which indigenous people were "pigeonholed into the socioeconomic category of *peasant*, a label that was even accepted by indigenous people themselves to overcome the baggage of disrespect and discrimination implied by previous terms[41]. The different descriptions which were created over time and which persist into the present day led to the creation of a wide-ranging set of identities, as described above.

While it was clear for the purposes of jurisprudence and legal doctrine, as well as for the academia, that both peasants and indigenous peoples had collective rights and were ensured protection under the law[42], the name or

---

40   Valencia/Egido 2010.
41   Albó 2002: 236.
42   In Bolivia, the Constitutional Tribunal has affirmed that the term "peasant" does not prevent any populations currently using the term from also considering

term had been cause for division among indigenous peoples during political processes over the last fifty years.

This chapter must omit a number of necessary clarifications on "culture," "class" and "ethnicity," and even more importantly the constant tension among these elements[43], in order to focus exclusively on the object of analysis: the terms or names that reflected the imagined identity causing division among the members of the Pact.

In referring to this phenomenon, it is important to start from the affirmation that language does not only describe reality, but also creates it[44]. In other words, the names given to objects in our surroundings serve to outline reality as we know it. In general, the more differences we can find in our reality, the more names we give. In social processes, specifically the relationship between people or groups of people, a similar situation occurs. The name creates an identity that distinguishes one person or group from the others.

It was implementing the process in reverse that involved Knowledge Sharing in the issue of resolving the conflict of identities and terms between members of the Pact. In other words, a name was created to downplay differences and create a new reality (in this case a creature).

"One subject with three names" or "three names for a single subject"

To understand the context that gave rise to the creation of the "creature," three aspects must first be highlighted:

- Within the Pact, the conflict over access to natural resources and land rights between Lowland indigenous communities and colonist "peasants", mentioned above, was clearly reflected. In addition, another conflict was going on between "first peoples'" and "peasants'" organisations from the Highlands over the political representation of the populations in their territories. In the latter conflict, the first peoples accused

---

themselves indigenous peoples, especially given that the term "peasant" was used by communities as a way of escaping discrimination, although they continued to live according to their own traditions and customs (Tribunal Constitucional de Bolivia 2006: 29).

43   For further reading: Salvador Schavelzon (2013) provides a worthwhile analysis of these elements.

44   Maturana 1997.

"peasants" of organizing themselves into structures and categories inherited from the "internal colonialism"[45] of the Republic. The "peasants" maintained that the term did not prevent them from simultaneously identifying as indigenous peoples.

- In many situations the "indigenous peoples" of the Lowlands found themselves at a disadvantage during Pact debates, due to both representing organisations with minority populations, and their minority presence within the configuration of the Pact itself – not to mention their insistence on using the term ("indigenous peoples") from which other groups sought to distance themselves.

- Small alliances were created during the heat of debate: one comprising "peasants" organisations, the other made up of organisations calling themselves "indigenous" and "first peoples". Once these two blocks were formed, the debate took on a different level of intensity.

The path (procedure) toward achieving agreement by externalizing and internalizing knowledge can be summarized as follows, in accordance with the conditions proposed by Ulrich Müller[46].

---

45 The term "internal colonialism" is a concept developed in the 1960s by two Mexican authors, Pablo Gonzales and Rodolfo Stavenhagen (Casanova 1963; Stavenhagen 1963). Within the framework of studying the condition of the subaltern and critiquing capitalism, they studied the relationships of dominance within States by the bourgeoisie and landowning classes over indigenous, rural and marginalized populations, as a synthesis of those passing between the *central* and the *peripheral* spheres of the global context. In other words, this concept has a clearly anti-capitalist political connotation, based in Marxist theory.

46 See chapter 2 in this volume by Ulrich Müller.

Table 1: Steps for making knowledge available to others as part of Knowledge Sharing processes

Self-reflection	Common reflection	Common language and sense of cooperation	Method
As described above, each organization had a logic supporting the identity that lay behind its name. This logic was brought into question when most of the participants affirmed that the majority of problems addressed by the Pact Proposal were of common interest, with similar alternatives for solution being proposed. (Valencia/Egido 2010; Garcés 2013).	The affirmation that representatives from each of the Pact's organizations shared a common history and future, which led to the reflection on having a common name that reflected all identities.	Making a comparison with the identity of a person with more than one name, intense debates were followed by an agreement that commas and conjunctions would be removed from the identities of Pact members. The creation of a trifurcated name –indigenous peasant first peoples ("indígena originario campesino" in Spanish) – was the Pact's most creative innovation.	With this agreement, other conflicts between Pact members were gradually smoothed – for example, those regarding collective land rights, or the processes of indigenous autonomy within Bolivia being among the most important (Valencia/Egido 2010; Garcés 2013). The common identity, in the common name, shifted debates from the level of negotiating positions to one of exchanging life experiences and knowledge. In other words, a process of Knowledge Sharing emerged when participants began to see one another as equals.

Source: Created by author

The Pact's Proposal achieved two main results in the process of drafting the constitution: first, the characterisation of Bolivia as a Plurinational State, unified but incorporating autonomous groups based on the principle of pluralism (art. 1); second, the recognition of the pre-existence of indigenous peoples and their territorial domain prior to the establishment of the colony (art. 2).[47]

Effectively, these two articles of the Political Constitution of the State (PCS) paved the way toward recognition of the collective rights of indigenous peoples ("pueblos indígena originario campesinos" in Spanish) to self-determination, political participation, prior consultation, administration of justice, use and possession of natural resources, and so on; it also solidified their individual rights based on their equality to the rest of the Bolivian population.

The implementation gap: Implementation of the Constitution

The implementation of the Constitution is a story of its own that continues to unfold. It is characterized on one hand by distancing of members of the Pact, the tension between the text of the Constitution and the current government's political agenda (which has gone about weakening many of the institutions which guarantee respect and protection of the rights contained in the PCS); and on the other by the configuration of new alliances, not only among indigenous groups but also between the latter and other sectors of the Bolivian population, and new ways of understanding wellbeing (or "living well," embodied in the phrase *"buen vivir"*) as a common good for all.

This story will be the focus of another text, perhaps in a context separate from Knowledge Sharing, unless those involved promote yet another process of externalizing and internalizing their knowledge and aspirations to the others.

Conclusions

Knowledge Sharing as a process that makes knowledge available to others is also a useful approach to processes of political dialogue and understanding; this is even more the case when there is a common project or interest

---

47   Valencia/Egido 2010; Garcés 2013.

between parties, as was the case with the Unity Pact of the Bolivian constituent process.

One basic condition for Knowledge Sharing is to enable parties to see one another as equals and the legitimacy of one another's positions or opinions. From another perspective, parties must identify the "mutual necessity" of legitimizing the other as a free agent with his or her own needs. As such, the principle of equality is not only the objective of Knowledge Sharing, but is also an essential condition in order for it to occur. In other words, Knowledge Sharing aids in finding one's own image in the face of the other.

In the case of the Unity Pact in Bolivia, finding such a context of equality was no easy task, but this achievement led to positive changes in the relationships between the actors within the Pact. As such, it allowed actors to shift from a position of negotiation and mutual distrust to one of trust and joint negotiation before a larger group.

References

Albó, Xavier (2008): Movimientos y poder indígena en Bolivia, Ecuador y Perú, CIPCA La Paz.

Agrawal, Arun (2002): Indigenous knowledge and the politics of classification, in: International Social Science Journal, Vol. 54(173), pp. 287 – 297. Accessible under: https://dx.doi.org/10.1111/1468-2451.00382 (11.05.2017).

Bartra, Roger (2014): Antropología del lenguaje. Conciencia, cultura y libre albedrío. Fondo de Cultura Económica Mexico.

Bateson, Gregory (1972): Steps to an Ecology of Mind. Collected Essays in Anthropology, Psychiatry, Evolution, and Epistemology. University of Chicago Press, Chicago.

Bethell, Leslie (ed.) (1991): Historia de América Latina. Ed. Crítica, Barcelona.

Camelo, Carmen/García-Cruz, Joaquín/Sousa, Elena (2010): Facilitadores de los procesos de compartir conocimiento y su influencia sobre la innovación, Cuadernos de economía y dirección de la empresa CEDE, Vol. 13(42), pp. 114-150.

Casal Hernández, Jesus María (2010): El constitucionalismo latinoamericano y la oleada de reformas constitucionales en la región andina, Rechtsgeschichte, Vol. 16(2010), Max-Planck-Instituts, München. Accessible under: http://dx.doi.org/10.12946 /rg16/212-241 (11.05.2017).

Casanova, Pablo González (1963): Sociedad plural, colonialismo interno y desarrollo. América Latina, Revista del Centro Latinoamericano de Investigaciones en Ciencias Sociales, Mexico City, Vol. VI(3).

Garcés, Fernando (2013): Los indigenas y su Estado (pluri)nacional: una mirada al proceso constituyente boliviano. JAINA FHyCE, UMSS CLACSO, Cochabamba.

Gómez, Augusto (1991): Indios, colonos y conflictos. Una historia regional de los Llanos Orientales. 1870 – 1970, XXI edition, Pontificia Universidad Javeriana y Siglo, Bogota.

Grenier, Louise (1998): Working with Indigenous Knowledge. A guide for researchers, International Development Research Centre (IDRC), Ottawa.

Gros Espiell, Héctor (2002): El constitucionalismo latinoamericano y la codificación en el siglo XIX, Centro de estudios Políticos y Constitucionales, Anuario Iberoamericano de Justicia Constitucional, No. 6, Madrid, pp. 143-175. Doi:10.18042/cepc/aijc

Iturralde, Diego (1995): La gestión de la multiculturalidad y la multietnicidad en América Latina, Debate Documents, No. 5, UNESCO. Accessible under: http://digital-library.unesco.org/shs/most/gsdl/cgi-bin/library?e=q-000-00---0most--00-0-0--0prompt-10---4----dtx--0-1l--1-en-50---20-about-conocimiento+ind%C3%ADgena--00031-001-1-0utfZz-8-00&a=d&c=most&cl=search&d=HASH01d0fb5 79eaf69dcc93f9958 (01.26.2016).

Leach, Melissa/Fairhead, James (2002): Manners of contestation: "citizen science" and "indigenous knowledge" in West Africa and the Caribbean, in: International Social

Science Journal, Vol. 54(173), pp. 299 - 311, Accessible under: https://dx.doi.org/ 10.1111/1468-2451.00383 (11.05.2017).

Luna de Sola, David (1978): Algunos aspectos ideológicos de la independencia latinoamericana, Anuario de Estudios Centroamericanos, Vol. 4(1978), pp. 79-92.

Mansilla, Hugo Celso Felipe (2014): La influencia del indianismo en la Asamblea Constituyente boliviana de 2006-2008. Observaciones críticas sobre la persistencia de una cultura política tradicional, Revista Estudios Políticos, Mexico City, Vol. 9(33), pp. 97-121.

Maturana, Humberto (1997): La objetividad – Un argumento para obligar, Dolmen Ed.: Santiago de Chile.

Paz, Octavio (1989): Piedra de sol, in: Paz, Ocatavio: El fuego de cada día. Selección, Seix Barral, Barcelona, pp. 85-100.

SAB-UNGA (Scientific Advisory Board of Secretary-General of the United Nation) (2016): Indigenous and Local Knowledge(s) and Science(s) for Sustainable Development, Policy Brief by the Scientific Advisory Board of the UN Secretary-General, SC/2016/UNSAB/ILK. Accessible under: http://unesdoc.unesco.org/ images/0024/002461/246104E.pdf (10.20.2016).

Schavelzon, Salvador (2013): El nacimiento del Estado Plurinacional de Bolivia – Etnografía de una Asamblea Constituyente, Plural Ed./CLACSO, La Paz.

Stavenhagen, Rodolfo (1963): Clases, colonialismo y aculturación. América Latina, Revista del Centro Latinoamericano de Investigaciones en Ciencias Sociales, Río de Janeiro, Vol. VI(4).

Tribunal Constitucional de Bolivia (2006): Sentencia Constitucional 0045/2006. Expediente: 2005-12440-25-RDI. Accessible under: https://buscador.tcpbolivia.bo/ (S(mmrvv3kary0snztmg4lzqavc))/WfrJurisprudencia.aspx (11.05.2017).

United Nations DESA (Department of Economic and Social Affairs) (2009): State of the World's Indigenous Peoples ST/ESA/328, United Nations publication, New York.

UN (United Nations) (2007): UN Declaration on the Rights of Indigenous Peoples, Art. 31. Accessible under: http://www.un.org/esa/socdev/unpfii/documents/DRIPS_ es.pdf (10.20.2016).

UNESCO (United Nations Educational, Scientific and Cultural Organisation) (2001): Universal Declaration on Cultural Diversity. Accessible under: http://unesdoc. unesco.org/images/0012/001271/127162e.pdf (10.20.2016).

— UNESCO-CIRAN (United Nations Educational, Scientific and Cultural Organisation – Centre for International Research and Advisory Networks) (2003): Best practices on Indigenous Knowledge. Accessible under: http://www.vcn.bc.ca /citizens-handbook/unesco/most/bpindi.html (10.20.2016).

— (2005): Convention on the Protection and Promotion of the Diversity of Cultural Expressions. Accesible under: http://portal.unesco.org/es/ev.php-URL_ID=31038 &URL_DO=DO_TOPIC&URL_SECTION=201.html (10.20.2016).

— (2015): UNESCO Science Report. Towards 2030. Accessible under: http://unes doc.unesco.org/images/0023/002354/235406e.pdf#235444 (10.20.2016).

Vadillo, Alcides (2009): Conflictividad agraria en Santa Cruz. El caso de San Julián-El Puente. Agua, tierra, minería y bosques, Programa de las Naciones Unidas para el Desarrollo, La Paz.

Valencia, María del Pilar/Egido, Iván (2010): Los Pueblos Indígenas de Tierras Bajas en el Proceso Constituyente Boliviano. Nuevos sueños y desafíos para solucionar viejos problemas. CEJIS, IWGIA, AECID & HIVOS, Santa Cruz.

World Bank (2015): Report Nº 93666-GLB. Program document for a dedicated grants mechanism for indigenous peoples and local communities (DGM) including a Strategic Climate Fund (SCF). Forest Investment Program grant in the amount of US$ 4.73 Million to Conservation International Foundation, USA for a global learning and knowledge exchange project (January 26, 2015). Accessible under: http://documents.worldbank.org/curated/en/853221468165866998/pdf/936660PGD 0P128010 Box385413B00OUO090.pdf (05.26.2016).

Navigating the Perfect Storm: The Contribution of Knowledge Sharing to Building Economic Resilience in Caribbean Nations

Iván Roberto Sierra Medel

The aftershocks of the international financial crisis that began in 2008 have dealt a severe blow to countries around the globe, as depressed levels of demand in the markets hurt trade, posing significant obstacles to industrialized nations and emerging economies struggling to energize their growth rates. By 2016, global Gross Domestic Product (GDP) remained below its potential to such a degree that proposals were touted to abandon it as a suitable metric to assess humanity's ability to make inroads into prosperity[1].

The Western Hemisphere, home to established economic powers the United States and Canada, as well as large emerging economies such as Brazil and Mexico, has struggled with disappointing growth rates for almost a decade, with very few nations (Panama and to some degree Peru) achieving annual rates of GDP expansion above the 5% mark for sustained periods[2]. The region located at the very core of the Continent, the Greater Caribbean, has been burdened with the most entrenched economic slowdown, diminishing the prospects of a better life for its young population.

This essay will make the case that the current situation affecting Caribbean countries as a region is characterized by the complex convergence of harsh economic realities, political factors, and social trends that present profound challenges to national governments. In this context, there is a need for innovative instruments of international development cooperation in order to carry out the strategic interventions that are required to jumpstart change. The text is structured in three sections. The first one highlights some of the most pressing issues that undermine the economic development of Caribbean nations. The second part discusses recent experiences of international development cooperation interventions in the area, focusing on traditional approaches that have shown some success. It should be noted that the effectiveness of the latter must entail avoiding constraint of the full

---

1   The Economist 2016.
2   World Bank 2016.

potential of stakeholder collaboration toward knowledge-sharing actions, thereby encouraging exchanges of experiences and broader involvement in active partnerships, which are analysed in the third section. Finally, the text points to lessons learned and to the path ahead in the evolving practice of international development cooperation in the Caribbean.

The quest for capacity-building and economic growth within the Caribbean Community (CARICOM)

The 12 independent nations of the Anglophone Caribbean (Antigua and Barbuda, the Bahamas, Barbados, Belize, Dominica, Grenada, Guyana, Jamaica, Saint Lucia, St Kitts and Nevis, St Vincent and the Grenadines, and Trinidad and Tobago) are located over a wide territory that extends from the Eastern Seaboard of North America to the Amazonian forests, and feature a range of stark contrasts including in population size, from the 3 million inhabitants-strong Jamaica, to the modestly populated St Kitts and Nevis with 54,000 people. There are two continental countries (Belize and Guyana) bordering large neighbours, as well as small islands further away from markets. Resource-rich Trinidad and Tobago and tourism-attracting nations draw visible contrasts with smaller economies in a region characterized by big disparities in income: according to the World Bank, Antigua and Barbuda, the Bahamas, Barbados, St Kitts and Nevis, and Trinidad and Tobago have become high-income countries, while Guyana remains in the group of lower-middle income countries.

The shared traits of cultural tradition and regional insertion have been the drivers of continuous political dialogue to enhance economic collaboration. The process towards a Caribbean Community (CARICOM) began in 1973, and over the years the independent Anglophone nations have teamed up with Haiti, Dutch-speaking Suriname and the British Overseas Territory of Montserrat in the endeavour to build a Common Market and Single Economy which could thrive on member nations' complementarities and foster regional resilience[3].

The Treaty of Chaguaramas that established CARICOM was built on the political rapport among leaders of core member nations that had achieved independence in the decade leading up to 1973. The potential for improved economic collaboration among the newly-independent Caribbean nations, as well as for expanded trade with partners outside the region was greatly

---

3   CARICOM 2005.

enhanced by the implementation of trade preferences to access the European markets in the mid-1970s. The creation of the African, Caribbean and Pacific Group of States (ACP) in 1975 as a common platform for the economic dialogue with industrial economies in Europe attested to the concrete interests encompassing developing countries. In the case of the Caribbean countries, the rationale dates back to the accession of Britain to the European Economic Community in 1973 and the subsequent expansion of extra-regional dialogue and the energized economic engagement with countries that used to have traditional ties to the former colonial powers[4].

Table 1. Members of the Caribbean Community CARICOM

English-speaking countries	Antigua and Barbuda, the Bahamas, Barbados, Belize, Dominica, Grenada, Guyana, Jamaica, Saint Lucia, St Kitts and Nevis, St Vincent and the Grenadines, and Trinidad and Tobago
Dutch speaking member	Suriname
French- and Creole-speaking member	Haiti
British Overseas Territory	Montserrat

Source: CARICOM 2005

The convergence of the active political dialogue among Caribbean countries[5] and shared access to European trade preferences based on the Lomé Convention of 1975 provided the foundation for a multi-decade integration process aimed at cementing not only a Common Market, but a Single Economy in CARICOM. Thus, member nations expect the Common Market and Single Economy to help them navigate the uncertainties of the global economy.

The commodities boom that began in the early 2000s delivered significant benefits to oil exporters such as Suriname and Trinidad and Tobago, as well as to gold-producing Guyana and bauxite-mining Jamaica[6]. The rise of standards of living and fiscal respite in countries that export raw materi-

---

4   Perez Bravo/Sierra Medel 1999.
5   CARICOM Heads of Government hold summits twice a year.
6   Caribbean Development Bank 2016.

als was coupled in the Caribbean with the reaping of business in international tourism and financial services by a number of English-speaking countries that succeeded in building entire offshore industries after the 9/11 attacks in the United States prompted the American government to enact stricter oversight of domestic banking operations[7].

The twin bouts of prosperity that overlapped across the Caribbean for the best part of a decade were instrumental in cushioning the adverse impact of external shocks in strategic sectors, most notably the spike in the price of cereals and other staples that began in 2007[8]. Preventing drastic price fluctuations and assuring an adequate supply of the goods included in the basic needs basket are of critical importance in the face of social ills that could easily be compounded by economic hardship, such as gang proliferation, drug-trafficking, and the prevalence of violent crime[9].

The relatively long period of sustained increase in per capita income in several Caribbean nations led to nominal Gross National Income (GNI) levels above US$12,736, the World Bank threshold for classification of countries in the high-income category, making them ineligible for traditional concessionary financing[10]. However, this rigid classification by nominal income does not necessarily reflect the fuller picture of the actual economic strengths and structural factors affecting a country. In the Caribbean, vulnerability to natural disasters (compounded by the effects of climate change) is probably one of the main constraints obstructing a nation's path towards development. One of the most dramatic examples of such vulnerability was seen in December 2013, when sudden downpours caused unprecedented devastation in three middle-income island nations: Dominica, Saint Lucia, and St Vincent and the Grenadines. Less than two years after that, tropical storm Erika brought such damage to Dominica in August 2015 that the country's government declared that the impact of the natural disaster could set Dominica's development back two decades[11].

As the international prices of commodities peaked in the early 2010s and began a rapid decline, major exporters of raw materials in the Caribbean

---

7   Sanders 2017.
8   CARICOM estimates that, taken as a group, its member countries import more than US$4 billion of food products every year.
9   According to the United Nations Office on Drugs and Crime (UNODC), Jamaica had the world's highest murder rate in 2008. Belize ranked 3rd highest in 2015.
10   Antigua and Barbuda, the Bahamas, Barbados, St Kitts and Nevis, and Trinidad and Tobago are considered high-income countries.
11   The Guardian 2015.

faced profound financial challenges. By 2016, importers in Trinidad and Tobago, a regional oil power, were facing an acute shortage of foreign exchange[12]. Suriname, which exports mainly bauxite, gold and oil, was prompted to enter negotiations with the International Monetary Fund (IMF) in 2016 in order to obtain financial assistance[13].

One of the key assumptions regarding the benefits of the economic integration process for its members rests on the argument that some informal mechanisms for stabilisation could emerge within the Common Market and Single Economy, as some countries specialize in the export of services while others specialize in commodities. Thus, the negative effects of an external shock could in theory be expected to be limited to a particular sector or category of goods. The situation that emerged in the mid-2010s in the Caribbean, however, does not point to the economic decline being confined to specific countries, but rather to some form of contagion affecting those countries that rely on the export of services, especially financial services. The strategy of "De-Risking" implemented by major international banking institutions that withdrew from Caribbean markets and even cut corresponding banking relationships with businesses in the area poses severe challenges to countries heavily invested in financial services. The issue is now being addressed at the Heads of Government Conference level. Facing the convergence of diminished earnings for commodities exporters and the outright closure of traditional channels for financial business, CARICOM members are confronting a "perfect storm" – a large-scale threat to their economic prospects[14].

The recent economic downturn has not played well with the population of countries in the English-speaking Caribbean. Diminished expectations have probably influenced the outcome of a number of elections held across the region in 2015-2017. Out of a total of 8 Anglophone countries that held elections, only the voters in Belize, and St Vincent and the Grenadines returned the incumbent government, while governments were unseated in the Bahamas, Guyana, Jamaica, Saint Lucia, St Kitts and Nevis, and Trinidad and Tobago[15].

Disgruntled electorates are expected to be a feature of modern democracies and the ever present threat of electoral change can have the beneficial

---

12   The Trinidad Guardian 2016a.
13   Stabroek News 2016.
14   Jamaica Observer 2016.
15   Jamaica Observer 2017.

effect of improving government accountability. However, in some Caribbean countries the need for political solutions is not confined to the electoral arena and extends to the security realm. This means that authorities must also take into account intractable emerging threats, especially extremism-bred terrorism. According to several estimates, some 100 citizens of Trinidad and Tobago have travelled to the Middle East to join the so-called Islamic State[16].

Table 2. Unease in Paradise. Economic, Political, and Social Challenges Facing Caribbean Countries

Area of Risk	Main Highlights
Economic Stagnation	External Debts Exceeding 80% of GDP Average Annual Growth Rates under 3%
Political Unrest	6 Governments Voted Out of Office in 2015-2017
Weakened Social Fabric	Surging Rates of Homicide
Contagion of Extremist Trends	Caribbean Combatants Joining Islamic State Militias
Vulnerability to Natural Disasters	Hurricanes Setting Back Development in Small Islands

Sources: CDB 2016; World Bank 2015; Jamaica Observer 2017; UNODC 2014; The Trinidad Guardian 2016c; The Guardian 2015

In order to jointly address the economic, political, and social challenges facing the region, leaders of CARICOM made the decision to strengthen their integration process. The blueprint for a more structured interaction that could deliver better results to the region as a whole, as well as to individual countries, is the 2015-2019 CARICOM Strategic Plan aimed at building economic resilience, social resilience, environmental resilience, technological resilience, a stronger CARICOM identity and better governance. Coordinated foreign and external relations are seen as key elements in the endeavour to improve regional resilience[17].

---

16   The Trinidad Guardian 2016c.
17   CARICOM 2014.

152

Traditional practices and evolving partnerships to foster development in the Caribbean

A collaborative engagement with countries outside of the Caribbean, as well as focused interventions capable of mobilizing the resources of international development cooperation partners, have traditionally been of pivotal importance to CARICOM member nations, since, as a group, they have benefited from initiatives such as trade preferences granted by the European Community/European Union and access to finance on concessional terms, from the enactment of the 4th European Development Fund (EDF) in 1975 until the implementation of the 11th EDF 2014-2020[18]. Historically, external assistance has been highly regarded as a means to promote structural change and foster regional prosperity in the Caribbean. Besides established North-South mechanisms, emerging partnerships have proved valuable as instruments that assist Caribbean counties in coping with momentous situations such as a sudden deterioration in the terms of trade or a drastic surge of the price of oil.

In recent years, the most important intervention in support of oil-importing Caribbean countries has been the Venezuela-led PetroCaribe, a South-South initiative that proved a critical lifeline in the context of the seven-fold increase in the international price of oil from 2001 to 2008. The energy cooperation facility was established by the Venezuelan government in 2005 and expanded steadily to become a major cooperation mechanism[19].

With the exception of oil-exporting Trinidad and Tobago, every member of CARICOM became a beneficiary of PetroCaribe, whose concessional provisions are mostly contingent on the oil price being above US$50 dollars per barrel and include the financing of almost 50% of the oil bill, as well as barter schemes to settle accrued debt. Venezuela allocated to PetroCaribe some 242,000 barrels per day. During the long period of high international prices for oil before prices plunged in 2014, it was estimated that PetroCaribe had a nominal monetary impact in excess of US$10 billion per year, as the mechanism met 45% of the oil needs of beneficiary countries[20]. PetroCaribe's economic cooperation provided significant relief for the budgets of countries that, on average, had to devote 12% of GDP to pay for the oil

---

18   European Parliamentary Research Service (EPRS) 2014.
19   Sierra 2015.
20   PetroCaribe supplied up to 75% of the oil needs of some Caribbean countries.

bill. By 2014, PetroCaribe's beneficiary countries had accrued a US$11 billion outstanding debt to Venezuela's national oil company, Petróleos de Venezuela S.A. (PDVSA)[21]. That figure amounts to 8% of the beneficiary countries' GDP as a group. For some countries, that debt surpasses 20% of GDP.

Several PetroCaribe beneficiary nations have opted to buy some of their accrued debt to the mechanism at a discount. In January 2015, the Dominican Republic raised US$1.9 billion in the financial markets and used the proceeds to redeem almost all of its accumulated stock of US$4.1 billion debt to PetroCaribe. The steep discount achieved by purchasing accrued nominal debt delivers an immediate benefit to the financial prospects of the country and may additionally result in fewer political constraints. The political aspects of the mechanism of Economic Cooperation among Developing Countries can be illustrated by the suspension of oil shipments to Guyana in the context of the hardening political discourse of the Venezuelan government toward the new Guyanese administration[22].

Political conditionality is but one of the factors preventing Caribbean countries from accessing existing international cooperation programs. The parallel dilemma of the automatic exclusion of countries with nominally high income from the major sources of concessional financing may even compound the unfavourable situation for the small economies in the region. In the context of the clear need for more appropriate strategies, innovative efforts by both established donors and emerging development partners come at a premium since they may inject much-needed flexibility and more comprehensive approaches in order to deliver effective results.

Mexico, a country with extensive experience as both recipient country and donor, embarked on an ambitious modernisation of its international development institutions when the International Development Cooperation Act came into force in April 2011. A few months later, in December 2011, the President of Mexico issued a Decree to provide a financial vehicle for economic cooperation activities in Central America and the Caribbean: the Financial Cooperation Strategy with Meso-American and Caribbean Countries, known as the Yucatan Decree (Acuerdo de Yucatán). The Strategy's financial facility can fund technical cooperation projects, economic collaboration, and can give grants and issue loans on concessional terms. In order

---

21   PetroCaribe 2014.
22   Stabroek News 2015b.

to allocate a budget to the Strategy, the Ministry of Finance has a dedicated monetary facility, known as the Yucatan Fund[23].

The Fund became operational in 2012, with an initial allocation of US$166 million. The Fund built partnerships with the United Nations Office for Project Services (UNOPS) and the Bank for Central American Integration to act as financial intermediaries in the region, and began the assessment of projects for a new portfolio. The first infrastructure projects were launched in Belize (customs facilities) and Nicaragua (highway construction). In its initial phase, the Fund committed financing for projects across Central America, as well as in a number of Caribbean countries, such as Belize, Granada, Jamaica, Haiti, and Saint Lucia[24]. The contemporary Mexican approach to International Development Cooperation shows greater flexibility in grant-making, especially for humanitarian purposes: in 2014, Mexico gave a US$1.5 million grant to alleviate the plight of the population affected by unusually heavy rain in Saint Lucia, Dominica, and St. Vincent and the Grenadines.

The feasibility of financial interventions in more flexible terms has prompted the introduction of new grant-allocating mechanisms by established donors. The United Kingdom, a traditional development partner of Caribbean nations, devised an innovative facility, the UK Caribbean Infrastructure Partnership Fund (UKCIF), announced by Prime Minister David Cameron in September 2015. The considerable financial clout of the UKCIF, which aims at disbursing US$550 million between 2016 and 2020, has made Britain the largest bilateral donor to the region[25].

In order to make the UKCIF operational, the British government entered an agreement with the Caribbean Development Bank, as the 8 Caribbean countries (Antigua and Barbuda, Belize, Dominica, Grenada, Guyana, Jamaica, Saint Lucia, St. Vincent and the Grenadines) designated as beneficiary nations of the fund together with one British Overseas Territory (Montserrat) are borrowing members of the Carribean Development Bank (CDB).

While the immediate policy mandate that the British government set for UKCIF is to fund infrastructure projects, there are a number of broader goals that the initiative may accomplish, such as enhancing job opportunities at the local level, fostering prosperity, reinforcing poverty eradication

---

23   Sierra 2014.
24   AMEXCID 2016.
25   Kaieterur News 2017.

efforts, improving resilience to climate change, and ensuring better access to basic services for the population.

Besides its stalwart external assistance to Caribbean countries, the UK has been invested in facilitating the development dialogue between the European Union and the Caribbean Region. For international cooperation purposes and trade facilitation, CARICOM members were joined by the Dominican Republic to create the Carribean Forum (CARIFORUM) as a more inclusive group that serves as a dialogue platform with the EU. The main facility set up by the European institutions to allocate funds to initiatives implemented in Caribbean nations is the Caribbean Regional Indicative Programme (CRIP) within the EDF[26]. The 10th EDF CRIP was signed in 2015 and includes commitments to provide US$400 million from 2014 to 2020. The main areas that the current CRIP addresses include regional economic integration and cooperation, climate change, disaster management, environment and sustainable energy, and crime and security. A distinctive feature of the CRIP-supported portfolio of projects is its focus on capacity-building actions at the national level that include in their core design elements related to regional capacity-building.

At the bilateral level, the European Union may extend assistance in the form of budgetary support to a number of countries in the Caribbean such as Guyana, the English-speaking country with the lowest per capita income in the Western Hemisphere. In order to obtain budgetary support, either in the form of General Budget Support or via Sector Budget Support, the recipient country has to meet eligibility criteria related to public finance management, accountability and transparency. In the case of Guyana, the European Union implements two budgetary support programs. The largest facility (US$40 million) is earmarked for the sugar sector, while a smaller fund (US$18 million) focuses on the country's sea defence[27].

Norway has expanded its development financing dialogue with selected countries in the context of the Nordic nation's policy to promote sustainable development as the best strategy to fight climate change. In 2009, Norway approached Guyana, the country with the largest territory in CARICOM and the one with the most extensive forest cover in order to build a partnership in climate change and forestry. By preventing deforestation in thinly-populated Guyana (whose economy by itself has a very small carbon footprint), and especially by expanding the infrastructure to harness clean

---

26   EPRS 2014.
27   Guyana Times 2015.

sources of energy, Norway can steer a comprehensive implementation of the REDD+[28] strategies and commitments emanating from the global talks to combat climate change.

The Norway-Guyana partnership includes the allocation of US$250 million. It has been reported that the Norwegian government deposited US$70 million in the Guyana REDD+ Investment Fund (GRIF), which is administered by the World Bank. An additional sum of US$80 million is held at the Inter-American Development Bank (IADB) in a special facility earmarked for the construction of a major hydropower dam in the Guyanese hinterlands at Amaila Falls. The combination of protected forestry and a transition to hydropower can set a successful example of green development strategy in an emerging economy[29].

The quest for extra-regional partnerships by CARICOM members can be illustrated by the growing relationship with the Islamic Development Bank (IsDB). In 2016, Guyana was formally inducted into the IsDB. Guyana and Suriname are the only two countries of the Western Hemisphere that participate in the Organisation for Islamic Cooperation (OIC) and both nations have achieved borrowing member status at the IsDB (Suriname's membership dates back to 1997). The potential benefits for the Caribbean countries are significant, as the IsDB's capital exceeds US$150 billion. The Bank provides grants and concessional loans in the areas of human development, rural development and food security, infrastructure, trade among member countries, research and development, and banking and finance[30].

---

28   REDD+ (Reducing Emissions from Deforestation and Forest Degradation and
      the Role of Conservation, Sustainable Management of Forests and Enhancement
      of Forest Carbon Stocks in Developing Countries).
29   Guyana Chronicle 2016c.
30   Kaieteur News 2016.

Table 3. Emerging Partners and Established Donors to the Caribbean

Flagship Programs in Economic Cooperation among Developing Countries	Major Initiatives by Traditional Donors	New Partnerships
Venezuela's PetroCaribe	United Kingdom's Caribbean Infrastructure program UKCIF	Norway's REDD+
Mexico's Acuerdo de Yucatan	European Union's (EU) EDF	Islamic Development Bank

Source: PetroCaribe 2014; Sierra 2015; CDB 2016; Guyana Chronicle 2016c; Kaieteur News 2016; EPRS 2014

While the allocation of financial resources on concessional terms and the proper monetisation of international development cooperation with the Caribbean as a whole are highly significant tasks, much-needed comprehensive capacity-building strategies require a wider approach. As third party expertise unleashes even more value when financial and technical resources foster a bi-directional interaction of stakeholders leading to actual knowledge-sharing, the next section addresses some current examples of good practices in knowledge-sharing in the Caribbean.

Good practices in knowledge-based cooperation

Economic cooperation interventions implemented in recent decades across the Caribbean make a significant contribution to the stability and growth prospects of the region. In a parallel process, development cooperation actions increasingly build partnerships enhanced by knowledge-sharing, an emerging practice whose basic tenets include the active engagement of development partners in order to adapt knowledge generated by others and to implement development solutions that have delivered results in other countries[31]. Such actions have relevant historical roots in the Caribbean, espe-

---

31   World Bank 2015.

cially among the region's English-speaking nations. Indeed, certain programs aimed at skills-development and human-resources training are seen as models of best practices in South-South Cooperation. One such example is the training of Nigerian medical students in Guyana[32].

Knowledge-based projects in the Caribbean have been better placed to make a significant contribution when their implementation addresses high-value areas, such as foreign language acquisition. As 17 million mostly Creole- and English-dominant nationals of CARICOM members come into close contact with the Greater Caribbean Basin with more than 200 million Spanish-speakers, Spanish language teaching provides relevant skills for young people in the Caribbean to reap economic opportunity. In this area, the Venezuelan Institutes for Culture and Cooperation established in CARICOM nations have for over 30 years been the major centres of learning[33]. Mexico has also made inroads in the area with some pilot programs to promote the acquisition of Spanish as a foreign language.

The specific approach of the Venezuelan Institutes for Culture and Cooperation has traditionally been student-centered, as they offer a curriculum that provides gradual advancement over a number of academic years. On the other hand, Mexico has focused on training secondary-level teachers of Spanish as a foreign language, selected by the governments of CARICOM member countries[34].

A key element of successful knowledge-sharing projects lies in their timely orientation towards strategic actions with the potential to spark transformational change. In this regard, South-South training and exchange of experiences may be conducive to inputs that lend themselves to more seamless appropriation by beneficiary countries than traditional North-South assistance. One example of that approach can be seen in Guyana, where U.S.-based ExxonMobil announced the discovery of considerable oil deposits in 2015. As Mexico has more than a century of experience in oil production, the Guyanese authorities began a partnership with Mexico in order to gain access to expertise to address high-priority areas of human resources training and the enactment of a comprehensive regulatory framework, both of which are urgently needed to jumpstart the development of a domestic oil industry in Guyana[35].

---

32   Guyana Chronicle 2016a.
33   Sierra 2015.
34   Stabroek News 2015a.
35   Stabroek News 2017.

China has emerged as a relevant actor in knowledge-sharing cooperation in the Caribbean region. Despite the formidable financial clout that allows Beijing to launch large grants such as the US$250 million earmarked for cooperation with the Community of Latin American and Caribbean Countries, the People's Republic of China faces a dilemma in its development cooperation relationship with the Caribbean region. Five CARICOM members (Belize, Haiti, Saint Lucia, St. Kitts and Nevis, and St. Vincent and the Grenadines) do not have diplomatic relations with the government in Beijing[36]. Lacking a political dialogue with more than a third of CARICOM member nations, China has diversified its international cooperation strategy and has expanded beyond traditional concessional funding and into a number of initiatives intended to promote confidence-building and goodwill.

The Chinese Medical Brigade ranks high among the knowledge-sharing, grassroots-level programs. The 12th Chinese Medical Brigade arrived in the Caribbean in June 2016 and includes 35 physicians, which specialize in the fields of acupuncture, anaesthesiology, gynaecology, nephrology, oncology, ophthalmology, radiology, obstetrics, paediatrics, surgery, and osteopathy. The benefits for the population in CARICOM countries are far-reaching. In Guyana, a country of 800,000 inhabitants, it is estimated that during the most recent visit by the Chinese Medical Brigade, the 11th Brigade treated 41,000 people, amounting to over 5% of the total population of the country[37].

Table 4. Knowledge-Sharing Development Partnerships in the Caribbean

Partner Country	Flagship Knowledge-Sharing Initiative in the Caribbean
Venezuela	Teaching of Spanish as Foreign Language to Students in Caribbean Countries at the Venezuelan Institutes for Culture and Cooperation
Mexico	Training of Secondary Level Teachers of Spanish Partnership for the Development of a Domestic Oil Industry in Guyana
China	Chinese Medical Brigades

Source: Sierra 2015; Stabroek News 2017; Guyana Chronicle 2016b

---

36   Council on Hemispheric Affairs 2012.
37   Guyana Chronicle 2016b.

As the forces of globalisation exert pressure on individual countries and put a premium on reinforcing competitiveness, CARICOM member nations have not only gone beyond the traditional issues of dismantling trade barriers, but have promoted innovative inroads in South-South Cooperation, especially actions pertaining to knowledge-sharing cooperation among Anglophone countries.

Among the areas that clearly demand targeted international cooperation interventions, the structural transformation of uncompetitive legacy industries in the Caribbean deserves special attention. Sugar-cane cultivation and sugar production are often mentioned as priorities in traditional sugar-exporting countries. In order to transform a troubled sector, the sugar industry requires a combination of concessional financial assistance and knowledge-sharing interventions involving relevant know-how. The Frome Sugar Estate in Jamaica provides a glimpse into the urgent task of improving productivity, as in 2016 the factory hit a 100-year low in its production of sugar, having produced 27,507 tons for the crop year. In contrast, a factory of similar size in Belize was producing 130,000 tons of sugar for the crop year[38].

In the area of education, the Caribbean standardized school examinations administered by national authorities under the coordination of the Caribbean Examinations Council or CXC have become the main instrument for regional cooperation[39]. The CXC tests assess the knowledge of students in primary and secondary schools and make a significant contribution to the regional endeavour to provide better education to the overwhelmingly young populations[40]. The favourable impact of accredited standardized tests on tertiary education and the job market has prompted non-CARICOM Anglophone nations to join the mechanism. Currently, the CXC council has 16 members (the entire English-speaking membership of CARICOM plus Anguilla, British Virgin Islands, Cayman Islands, and Turks and Caicos Islands).

CARICOM, whose secretariat is located in Guyana, has established specific agencies to facilitate knowledge-sharing among members, such as the Caribbean Environmental Health Institute (CEHI), whose work focuses on environmental management. CEHI fosters the exchange of experiences in areas that have a direct impact on climate change mitigation (energy effi-

---

38   The Gleaner 2016.
39   The CXC is a CARICOM institution established in 1972.
40   CXC 2016.

ciency, transport, waste management) as well as adaptation (water management, agriculture, institutional framework). In its effort to enhance capacity-building in strategic areas, CEHI joins partnerships with agencies such as United Nations Environmental Programme (UNEP), as it did in the execution on the project on Integrating Watershed and Coastal Area Management (IWCAM) in the Small Island Developing States of the Caribbean[41].

The path ahead

The challenges facing the Caribbean countries in the economic, political, and social dimension are manifold and demand effective responses that should be multi-faceted and align the expectations of diverse stakeholders – most importantly, those of the young population in CARICOM nations. Since the lack of sufficient economic dynamism in countries across the region is related to the overreliance on traditional sectors struggling to cope with globalisation, as well as with the heavy toll exacted by a range of natural disasters, the fundamental burden lies with the region's unusually high level of vulnerability. For that reason, the argument can be made that the engine best suited to navigating the perfect storm should be the multi-actor resilience-building on an individual country level, as well as in the region as a whole.

In the quest to make better use of scarce financial, material, and human resources, some large donors have adhered in recent years to a point of view that differentiates (critics might say "discriminates against") developing countries with supposedly enough domestic resources to jumpstart development solutions and countries in actual need of external assistance. A rigid compact of development cooperation that allows, and indeed advocates for, the exclusion of some countries because they have surpassed a rigid threshold of per capita income does not serve the interests of development partners, for it ignores the potential perpetuation of stunted growth.

A more nuanced and pragmatic approach to the required partnerships, coupled with the allocation of adequate resources, has produced interventions in capacity-building that meet the local demands and are better able to mobilize the potential for focused solutions. No country in the Caribbean, regardless of per capita income, is above the objective need for more robust infrastructure and a better-trained workforce, and financial assistance that does not exclude grants and loans in concessional terms deserves a place

---

41   Ngoka 2016.

among best practices in the area of results-oriented international development cooperation interventions.

A multi-stakeholder political commitment to scaling-up international cooperation programs in the Caribbean may yet be the best strategy for both industrialized nations and developing countries in the region to implement in order to address specific issues in capacity-building aimed at strengthening regional competitiveness and also to counterbalance uncertainty. This endeavour suddenly became even more relevant after June 23rd, 2016, when voters in the United Kingdom decided that their country should opt out of the European Union (the Britain's Exit or "Brexit" referendum). As shockwaves of instability affected financial markets around the world, Caribbean leaders began a process of regional consultations to assess the potential impact that the loss of the British voice and vote in European institutions and policy-making bodies could have for the EU-CARICOM relationship[42]. Since English-speaking countries in the Caribbean have benefited from an active dialogue with the UK as members of the Commonwealth, their special ties to Britain play a role in shaping the economic prospects of the region. As there is a real danger that the Brexit process might compound the perfect storm facing the Caribbean, the present situation should prompt development partners in the Western Hemisphere to take action and provide a timely response.

---

42   The Trinidad Guardian 2016b.

Bibliography

AMEXCID (Agencia Mexicana de Cooperación Internacional para el Desarrollo) (2016): Proyecto de Integración y Desarrollo de Mesoamérica. Años 2008-2015, AMEXCID, Mexico.

CDB (Caribbean Development Bank) (2016): 2015 Economic Review/2016 Forecast, CDB, Barbados, Bridgestown.

CXC (Caribbean Examinations Council) (2016): CXC History. Accessible under: http://www.cxc.org/ (10.25.2017).

CARICOM Secretariat (2005): CARICOM, Our Caribbean Community. An Introduction, Ian Randle Publishers, Kingston.

CARICOM Secretariat (2014): Strategic Plan for the Caribbean Community 2015-2019. Repositioning CARICOM, CARICOM, Guyana.

Council on Hemispheric Affairs (2012): China vs. Taiwan. Battle for Influence in the Caribbean. Accessible under: http://www.coha.org/ (10.25.2017).

EPRS (European Parliamentary Research Service (2014): European Development Fund. Joint development cooperation and the EU budget: out or in?, EPRS, Brussels.

Guyana Chronicle (2016a): Nigerian trainee doctors, nurses host empowerment session at Joshua House, Georgetown, 6.22.2016.

Guyana Chronicle (2016b): More Chinese doctors-12th Chinese Medical Brigade arrives, Georgetown, 6.16.2016.

Guyana Chronicle (2016c): Government commits to climate pact with Norway, Georgetown, 1.29.2016.

Guyana Times (2015): Guyana signs contract with EU to prep Govt. for budgetary support, Georgetown, 7.11.2015.

Jamaica Observer (2017): Opposition wins general election in in Bahamas-Christie concedes defeat, Kingston, 5.11.2017.

Jamaica Observer (2016): De-risking or destruction? Neither is fair, Kingston, 1.30.2016.

Kaieteur News (2016): Guyana, Islamic Development Bank explore means for cooperation, Georgetown, 10.20.2016.

Ngoka, Millie (2016): Integrating Watershed and Coastal Area Management in the Small Island Developing States of the Caribbean (IWCAM). Accessible under: http://old.iwlearn.net/iw-projects/1254 (10.25.2017).

PetroCaribe (2014): PetroCaribe Management. Report Quarter I. 2014, PDVSA, Caracas.

Pérez Bravo, Alfredo/Sierra Medel, Ivan (1999): Contemporary Trends in International Technical Cooperation, SRE-PNUD-Miguel Angel Porrúa, México.

Sanders, Ronald (2017): The Future of Financial Services in the Caribbean. International Tax Competition, Globalisation and Fiscal Sovereignty, Goethals Consulting Group, Panama.

Sierra Medel, Ivan (2014): Nuevos instrumentos para la cooperación entre países en desarrollo: el Acuerdo de Yucatán, in: Ayala Martínez, Citlali/Rivera de la Rosa Jesús (eds.): De la diversidad a la consonancia: La Cooperación Sur-Sur latinoamericana, Instituto Mora-BUAP-CONACYT, México, pp. 15-32.

Sierra Medel, Ivan (2015): International Development Cooperation. A Practitioner's Roadmap, Groppen, Mexico.

Stabroek News (2015a): Twenty-nine Caribbean teachers benefit from Spanish training, Georgetown, 12.20.2015.

Stabroek News (2015b): Rice deal to end in November-Venezuela tells Guyana, Georgetown, 7.10.2015.

Stabroek News (2016): Suriname considering approach to IMF, Georgetown, 1.25.2016.

Stabroek News (2017): Milestone agreement inked, Georgetown, 3.17.2017.

The Economist (2016): How to measure prosperity, London, 4.30.2016.

The Gleaner (2016): Sugar falls short-Frome factory produces record low for crop year. Kingston, 6.13.2016.

The Guardian (2015): Tropical storm Erika: Dominica declares disaster and seeks aid, London, 8.31.2015.

The Trinidad Guardian (2016a): Local businesses expecting more forex shortages. Port of Spain, 12.29.2016.

The Trinidad Guardian (2016b): Brexit fallout: Problems for trade, tourism in the Caribbean, Port of Spain, 6.26.2016.

The Trinidad Guardian (2016c): Government taking ISIS threat seriously-PM. Port of Spain, 5.26.2016.

UNODC (United Nations Office on Drugs and Crime) (2014): Global Study on Homicide 2013, UNODC, Vienna.

World Bank (2015): Scaling Up Knowledge–sharing for Development. A Working Paper for the G-20 Development Working Group, Pillar Nine, World Bank Group, Washington, D. C.

World Bank (2016): Global Economic Prospects 2016. Divergences and Risks, World Bank Group, Washington D.C.

Conclusions and Outlook

Citlali Ayala Martínez and Ulrich Müller

"I want to have that!"[1]

Knowledge Sharing has become an essential pillar for development cooperation, as well as for the achievement of global development goals recently summarized in the 2030 Agenda for Sustainable Development. It has even been said that the Agenda 2030 is a Knowledge Sharing Agenda[2]. Knowledge Sharing was a highly relevant factor for the preparation of the Agenda 2030 and will be necessary for its implementation. The cases studied in this book offer examples of how successful Knowledge Sharing initiatives help to further the global development agenda.

Participation through Knowledge Sharing

Knowledge Sharing has played a key role in deepening participation in the discussion of global development goals. While the Millennium Development Goals (MDG) were mainly an expert's product, the preparation of the Agenda 2030 gave room for participation by all countries, who brought their ideas to the negotiation of the agenda and left their specific marks on the process. A clear example of this is the proposal by the governments of Colombia and Guatemala[3] "that a key outcome of the Rio + 20 process be the definition and agreement of a suite of Sustainable Development Goals (SDG), similar and supportive of the MDG." This proposal was a landmark towards the integration of previously separate UN (United Nations) processes in the Agenda 2030.

---

1   This phrase was used several times during the knowledge sharing sessions of the International Symposium "Gießen local-global, New Views on Worldwide Partnership and Justice - Reformatory Challenges 2017", June 22-25, 2017, when participants from other countries presented their tools and approaches. The results of the event organized by the Protestant Deanery of Gießen have been incorporated into the following text.

2   GPKS 2016.

3   Ministerio de Relaciones Exteriores. República de Colombia 2012: 1.

While the idea of the Millennium Development Goals was to achieve improvements in developing countries, the Agenda 2030 is valid for all countries according to the principle of universality. Thus, all countries are considered as having some aspects to develop, and therefore find themselves on equal terms regarding the goals. This is an important step toward overcoming the ever present issue of "who is ahead," strengthening joint global responsibility. Therefore, development and innovation are no longer the purview, as Horacio Rodríguez points out, of "a 'creative' few".[4] Instead, development becomes a "collective act and the responsibility of all." Jointly, humankind is drawing attention to the future of our planet, its people – especially those with insufficient access to the goods and services they need – prosperity, peace and partnership. This corresponds with the idea of horizontal communication in Knowledge Sharing, making all parts involved learners and providers of knowledge.

In this regard, participation requires the ability both to articulate and make oneself heard, which is the typical notion of empowerment, and to acknowledge and promote agency[5]. The latter also requires standing back and loosening control[6]. As a consequence, both sides start to see one another as equals and to recognize "the legitimacy of one another's positions or opinions"[7]. This kind of self-reflection must then shift to a kind of "common reflection"[8], from an "attitude of openness towards diversity" to "co-creation".[9]

The Agenda 2030 is no longer a document imposed by a few rich and leading countries on many others. Therefore, it marks a completely new chapter in international cooperation. For the preparation of the Agenda, civil society, the academia and local administrations were consulted, which is another important change in comparison with the design process of the Millennium Development Goals. It is a step towards granting equal rights to societies, communities and local levels everywhere in the world, access to information and the opportunity to express opinions for everyone in every social group in an open communication without borders of geography, hierarchy or race. It is a movement for sharing not only knowledge, but also fears and concerns as well as respect and friendliness. Thus, room is open to redefine what development means.

---

4   Rodríguez: 114 in this book.
5   See the chapter of Horacio Rodríguez in this book, pp. 113-126.
6   See the chapter of Ulrich Müller in this book, pp. 43-66.
7   Égido: 142 in this book.
8   Ibid.: 137 in this book.
9   Müller: 44 in this book.

As has been shown, Knowledge Sharing is not only a means for participation in decision-making, but also a precondition for making this participation possible. A clear example is provided given by Iván Égido on the constitutional reform in Bolivia of 2009. Without Knowledge Sharing, the different indigenous groups and organisations in the country would not have been able to develop a coordinated message on their interests in the constitutional process. Marcela Morales and Melani Peláez[10] add an interesting observation in this context: experts' networks do not generally correspond to one single specific typology, but rather "hybrids" combining elements of advocacy networks and epistemic communities, in order to achieve their goals in participation for decision-making.

It should also be noted that participation and thereby the role of Knowledge Sharing does not end with the formulation of the Agenda 2030, but is also a basic requirement for its implementation. Here it is able to provide necessary changes not only at the level of persons but also within organisations and societies[11].

Beyond data reporting: real change

Of relevance to Knowledge Sharing in the Agenda 2030 is the measurement of progress in achieving the sustainable development goals. Monitoring and evaluation form an important part of the Agenda's means of implementation as set out in goal 17. Communication must include references to the achievements made towards the global goals in an impressive effort of data sharing. Despite the importance of data collecting, the real situations of people with little voice in international debates should not be neglected. Know-how and human needs have to "coincide in development solutions, by way of Knowledge Sharing, individual capacities and collective actions, as soon as they respond to public policies and national or local priorities"[12].

It also runs too short to categorize countries according to development indicators in order to define strategies, activities and partnerships.

---

10   See the chapter of Marcela Morales and Melani Peláez in this book, pp. 95-112.
11   See the chapter of Iris Barth, Ulrich Müller and Anna Fiedler in this book, pp. 67-94.
12   Ayala: 38 in this book.

"A rigid compact of development cooperation that allows, and indeed advocates for the exclusion of some countries because they have surpassed a rigid threshold of per capita income does not serve the interest of development partners"[13].

A closer look at the living conditions of people affected by poverty, vulnerable to environmental disasters and exposed to war and violence shows that differences are not always to be found where expected. There are many hybrid and mixed situations within countries, while country-to-country similarities open a wide field for exchange of experiences. Outsiders' views help to overcome deadlocks in which the usual partners are stuck, and to recognize situations and challenges with fresh and open eyes. This requires people able to "understand local realities" and "sensitized to the culture, ways and customs" of different communities[14], "a mix of personal competences in the partners involved, as well as openness and political will at an institutional and societal level" that allows creating a "Knowledge Sharing friendly ambience in organisations and societies, revising incentives as well as rules and regulations"[15]. In this way, debate shifts "from negotiating positions" to "exchanging life experiences and knowledge"[16].

Thus, real change is a matter of small steps within the concrete situations of people and environments, but also requires legal regulations, jointly agreed rules and standards. Both must go hand in hand in a bidirectional communication that assures recognition of local needs, as well as acceptance and fulfilment of standards and regulations. Hence, a bidirectional local to national and global Knowledge Sharing process must take place in order to achieve real change. Here, regional networks are essential

"in generating perspectives from the global south. Regional platforms ... have the ability and the potential to mobilize peers and partners to generate knowledge and create environments that are conducive to enhancing horizontal cooperation."[17].

Moreover, the "engine best suited to navigating the perfect storm" that currently shakes many countries in the world "should be the multi-actor resilience-building on an individual country level, as well as in the region as a whole"[18].

---

13   Sierra: 162 in this book.
14   Rodríguez: 122 in this book.
15   Müller: 62 and 63 in this book.
16   Égido: 140 in this book.
17   Morales/Peláez: 109 in this book.
18   Sierra: 162 in this book.

The local-global link

In order to achieve real change it is necessary to forge a connection between the local, national and global spheres. Here again, Knowledge Sharing has great potential. This is especially the case in terms of valuing local knowledge, individual capabilities and life experiences. This is also a key question facing the implementation of the Agenda 2030: Is it truly close enough to the reality of people in all countries? Does it inspire concrete action among local administrations, local civil society organisations, entrepreneurs, university teachers etc. going beyond that what has always been done before? Is it, for instance, sufficient to explain to students why the sustainable development goals are important and how poverty, environmental protection and human rights are connected? Is there a good reason to lean back and be content with what is already being carried out?

What can be expected from local administrations? Even in comparatively wealthy regions such as Europe or global centers such as Mexico City, they often complain about a lack of staff and funds and do not develop new solutions. And the almost omnipresent challenges of corruption and clientelism cannot be forgotten. Knowledge Sharing can supply local know-how, initiatives based on human skills, and thereby support solutions that become integrated into people's daily lives. In order for this to be achieved, sharing must go beyond intellectual insights and include practical abilities and attitudes[19]. For example,

> "Knowledge Sharing events with indigenous communities must give special relevance to the context and to local actors, promoting a territorial approach from a broader perspective, considering the physical, climate and agro-ecological characteristics of the territory, as well as ancestral wisdom, world view, culture and interactions between different actors (both public and private) within the local productive system"[20].

In order for change to be visible on the ground, meaningful links between several levels need to evolve, which respectfully connect global decision-making with local action, considering the potential and requirements of both.

---

19   See the chapter of Iris Barth, Ulrich Müller and Anna Fiedler in this book, pp. 67-94.

20   Rodríguez: 122 in this book.

Figure 1: The local-global link

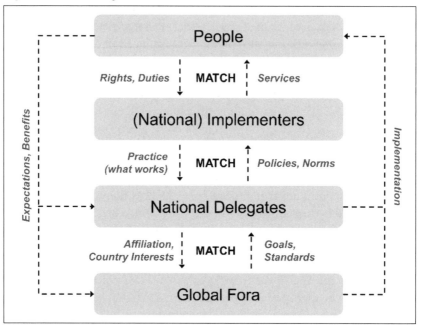

Source: Draft by the authors

Knowledge Sharing can be especially helpful for enhancing relationships between national governments and local action. Here, national implementers, either subnational governments, civil society or private enterprises, play a crucial role[21]. Their insights are gradually gaining in importance in global negotiations. Although it is generally known "that implementation and policy formulation are highly interdependent processes" and that "implementers are political actors in their own right"[22], the necessary negotiations between implementers and decision-makers at the national and global level still have to increase. Dialogues among people and organisations on different levels and among people and organisations at the same level – but in different places – demonstrate that Knowledge Sharing is an appropriate tool to be leveraged with different audiences. This means to "make improbable encounters happen and use their potential to combine existing knowledge into new answers and solutions"[23].

---

21   See the chapter of Citlali Ayala in this book, pp. 19-42.
22   Pülzl/Treib 207: 101 and 96 as cited in Ayala/Müller 2014: 41.
23   Müller: 63 in this book.

Processes such as these require clarity of roles and empowerment, not only of actors at different levels within the state but also among private enterprises and civil society organisations. Empowerment will always be a process that people and entities do for themselves. It cannot be done from outside. However, it is possible to create positive conditions for empowerment, for instance, by fostering people's self-reliance in overcoming paternalistic practices of assistentialism. This happens when people are consulted and encouraged but also confronted with the consequences of their actions. Empowerment means providing opportunities that fit the needs and abilities of people and organisations. Sharing ideas freely is an important element of empowerment. Horizontal dialogue creates self-esteem and self-reflection in order to develop personal, sector area, social and methodological competences[24]. Therefore, the process of Knowledge Sharing "should be focused on ensuring the creation, development and strengthening of local capacities, in order to enable ownership, shared responsibility and sustainability in innovation over time"[25].

Increased dialogue among practitioners

International development cooperation is very important to promote Knowledge Sharing for the achievement of the Agenda 2030. New perspectives view international development cooperation as not only a source of finance, but also an opportunity for peers to learn from one another – those who regularly meet in global fora and also, perhaps more importantly, those who act locally. It is an opportunity to address what is most useful from different worlds combining "what we learned from our grandparents" with "today's innovations"[26]. Each country, each city and village, each organisation and person is responsible for its contributions to the Sustainable Development Goals. However, development cooperation, inclusive alliances and mutual learning practices can give these actions the last push toward success[27]. Local actors can create structures that organize dialogue and Knowledge Sharing in simple and straightforward ways that do not require too much effort. This can also enhance joint and broader visions on the

---

24   See the chapter of Ulrich Müller in this book, pp. 43-66.
25   Rodríguez: 124 in this book.
26   Ibid.: 120 in this book.
27   See the chapter of Citlali Ayala in this book, pp. 19-42.

global goals and on international cooperation and should "be of concern to those moderating networks and the organisations participating in them"[28].

In Knowledge Sharing, persons have the opportunity to see reflections of themselves in others. Thus, they learn about themselves and empower through others. Knowledge Sharing "aids in finding one's own image in the face of the other"[29]. The perspective of outsiders is especially helpful in contexts where local people are stuck in challenges and conflicts and need to step back and take a different point of view. Knowledge Sharing can also be the starting point of joint action and working experiences. It helps to clarify self-concepts and work in and on the center of personal values.

Therefore, international exchange is increasingly necessary. This includes "networks of learning", "creation of public-private partnerships", "synergies with other institutions and organisations" or extension of communication "to large-scale channels" such as television and radio[30], but also digital platforms and social media. Thus, "collaborative networks for knowledge generation have the potential to transform think tanks into think-nets"[31].

Final considerations

It could be said that Knowledge Sharing has become the "third pillar" of development cooperation, as said by some practitioners[32], after technical and economic cooperation, as may be perceived throughout the diverse experiences reviewed in this book. Its potential is evident in a wide range of possibilities, from agriculture extension to a constitutional reform such as the Bolivian case. The world is currently in the process of bringing old beliefs and paradigms into question, as shown in "the perfect storm".

Working and thinking together is a more appropriate answer to new challenges than national selfishness and building walls. KS has demonstrated its potential to foster regional integration, to gather different idiosyncrasies, and to give individuals, organisations and societies the opportunity to learn and provide knowledge in a virtuous cycle of inputs and outputs.

---

28   Morales/Peláez: 110 in this book.
29   Égido: 142 in this book.
30   Rodriguez: 124 and 123 in this book.
31   Morales/Peláez: 102 in this book.
32   Schulz/Freire 2011.

The Giessen local-global event held in June 2017 in parallel to this publication provided nine theses for worldwide partnership and justice. As can be seen in Box 1, Knowledge Sharing is constantly in action, on demand and producing a diverse range of input for human development. The connections between different actors and levels is still a task to be improved, but a strong basis has been set for the way ahead.

Box 1: Gießen local-global: Nine theses for worldwide partnership and justice
1. Today's challenge is less to transmit knowledge but to share it. In order to achieve this, we must overcome the question of who is ahead, who is further developed. All experiences are good and valuable.
2. Differences are often not where we think. Many challenges are similar between countries although contexts are different. Therefore, joint learning is useful and necessary. On the other hand, there are great differences within countries. This makes it essential to have a closer look.
3. It is also important to think and act beyond the established divisions of sectors. All topics are interrelated. Therefore, in the same place we should know more about what is done in different fields of action.
4. When sharing and exchanging with others, especially from country to country and continent to continent, I see a reflection of myself and learn new things about myself. We always learn through others. When I am stuck, the other leads me out.
5. We empower ourselves and each other for dialogue and the sharing of knowledge, experiences, abilities and attitudes. Empowerment is the responsibility of each individual. However, we can create an ambience together that makes empowerment easier. This also means abstaining from creating dependencies, such as through the provision of aid.
6. Global goals have to become locally tangible. Global standards, national rules and small concrete local steps belong together. Global standards build upon local experiences. Meanwhile, small local steps must be embedded in broader contexts to become more than small steps.
7. It is important to communicate, and how we communicate, without limits of geography, hierarchy, race or religion. Our meetings and messages should based on respect and friendliness, and take fears and concerns seriously. We have the chance to experiment with

> working methods beyond the usual standards, which reach our hearts
> and allow connection with our daily actions.
>
> 8. We need more and different practices of global dialogue and new
>   forms of cooperation. To achieve this we can use the whole set of
>   media and methods available. Language does not need to be a barrier.
>   A lot can be transmitted without words. Many obstacles lie within
>   ourselves, when we are not open. Creativity is needed to make inter-
>   national encounters easy and low cost.
> 9. We have the chance to redefine what development means. We step
>   back from long-standing convictions. We talk about it, sing about it
>   and dance our successes.

It is possible to advocate for Knowledge Sharing as a task of all development actors, as a capability to be built among persons, organisations and
societies and also as a factor to foster governance frameworks and change
realities. The outcome is possible when development actors and decision
makers, productive and recording systems exercise agency for it. Today's
world demands agency and otherness, which is possible by the acknowl-
edgement of mutual capacities on development solutions.

Bibliography

Ayala Martínez, Citlali/Müller, Ulrich (2014): Implementation, Ownership, Cooperation as Challenges of Global Governance, in: Lázaro Rüther, Lena/Ayala Martínez, Citlali/Müller, Ulrich (eds.): Global Funds and Networks. Narrowing the Gap between Global Policies and National Implementation, Nomos, Baden-Baden, pp. 27-62.

Freres, Christian/Schulz, Nils-Sjard (2011): Emerging Lessons on Institutionalizing Country-Led Knowledge Sharing - G20 Issues Paper, World Bank Institute.

GPKS (Global Partnership on Knowledge Sharing) (2016): Towards Action on Country-led Solutions for Sustainable Development. Perspectives from the first meeting of the Global Partnership on Knowledge Sharing, World Bank. Accessible under: https://www.knowledgesharingfordev.org/Data/wbi/wbicms/files/drupal-acquia/wbi/document_repository/20160414_summary_gpks_meeting.pdf (11.09.2017).

Ministerio de Relaciones Exteriores. República de Colombia (2012): RIO + 20: Sustainable Development Goals (SDGs). A Proposal from the Governments of Colombia and Guatemala. Accessible under: http://www.stakeholderforum.org/fileadmin/files/Rio+20%20SDGs%20Colombia.pdf (06.26.2017).

About the Authors

Citlali Ayala Martínez is a Research Professor at the Research Institute Dr. José María Luis Mora (CONACYT) in Mexico-City. She holds a Bachelor's degree in International Relations and a Master's in Development Cooperation, and is currently a doctoral candidate in Political Science at the Technical University of Darmstadt in Germany. She was part of the Managing Global Governance Programme at the German Development Institute. Her areas of specialisation are cooperation among middle-income countries, South-South and triangular cooperation, as well as international cooperation in higher education and internationalisation processes. As a consultant on development cooperation, she has experience in South-South and Triangular Cooperation, as well as institutional strengthening processes in Central America, Mexico and Indonesia. She has many publications on development cooperation both as an editor and as an author. Email: cayala@mora.edu.mx

Iris Barth is a geographer from Philipps University Marburg, Germany, and holds a Master's degree in Peace Studies/Conflict Resolution. From 2001 to 2007, she worked with the Deutsche Gesellschaft für Internationale Zusammenarbeit (GIZ), first at the Head Office in Eschborn and later in Argentina as a project manager. After that, she continued in Argentina as an Integrated Expert (Centre for International Migration and Development, CIM/GIZ) at the National Research and Extension Institute for Agriculture, INTA. Iris has a broad knowledge about Latin American countries and since 2014, Iris has been working as a Buenos Aires-based freelance consultant. Her professional focuses include climate change, management of natural resources, result-based planning and monitoring and organisational development. She is highly experienced as a trainer and academic lecturer. Email: barth.iris@inta.gob.ar

José Iván Égido Zurita is an economist with a postgraduate degree (MA) in Human Rights and Governance (Universidad de Alcalá, Henares, Spain). He has extensive work experience with disadvantaged groups, such as indigenous peoples and small producers, in different Latin American countries, and has worked on children's and adolescents' rights and issues as well as gender equity. Iván has also worked and published on intercultural and transcultural issues, and earned a diploma (specialisation) as a mediator in intercultural conflicts (Pedagogical social training center of the State of Rheinland-Pfalz, Germany). Email: ivanegido@gmail.com

Anna Julia Fiedler is a graduate of East Asian Studies and Political Science from Free University Berlin (B.A.) and Leiden University (M.A. hons.). Her research focuses on social movements in greater China, particularly on discourse and network analysis. During a six-month internship at GIZ, she engaged in theories of networks and Knowledge Sharing in international cooperation. Email: annajuliafiedler@hotmail.com

Marcela Morales Hidalgo is the Research Coordinator for the Extractive Industries Program at Grupo Faro. She has worked on research projects relating to extractive industries and education in Latin America. She is currently engaged in researching local content as a development strategy in African and Latin American oil and gas producing countries as part of the ELLA Initiative. From 2008 to 2012, she worked at the United Nations Office on Drugs and Crime in Ecuador and the Global Outreach and Campaigns Department at Transparency International in Germany. Marcela holds an MA in Intercultural Conflict Management from Alice Salomon Hochschule in Germany and a BA in International Affairs and International Trade from the Catholic University of Ecuador (PUCE). Email: mmorales@grupofaro.org

Ulrich Müller holds a PhD in geography and specializes in development policies and governance. He joined the Deutsche Gesellschaft für Internationale Zusammenarbeit (GIZ) in 1997 and currently works as a Senior Advisor in the Division of Methodological Approaches where he focuses on Networks, Knowledge Sharing, Triangular Cooperation, Emerging Countries Cooperation Agencies and Development Funds. For over 30 years, he has worked with and in Latin America, particularly in Colombia, Argentina, Paraguay, Bolivia, Brazil and Mexico. He also co-edited a series of scientific books on development topics such as Ownership and Political Steering, Triangular Cooperation and Global Funds and Networks. He also collaborates regularly as a lecturer on development cooperation at the Technical University of Darmstadt (Germany) and at Instituto Mora in Mexico City. Email: ulrich.mueller@giz.de

Melani Peláez Jara is a researcher and PhD candidate in the Chair of Sustainability Governance of the University of Freiburg, Germany. She holds a Master's degree in Environmental Governance from the same university, having previously studied International Affairs and International Trade at the Catholic University of Ecuador (PUCE), and FLACSO-Ecuador. She has worked at Deutsche Gesellschaft für Internationale Zusammenarbeit (GIZ), the United Nations Environment Programme (UNEP), the former Exports Promotion Agency of Ecuador, and she has collaborated with Grupo FARO, Ecuador. Her professional and academic focus is on environmental and sustainability governance, international cooperation, and science and policy studies. Email: contact@melanipelaez.com

Horacio Rodríguez Vázquez holds a Master's degree in International Development Cooperation. His experience in international organisations is related to food security, rural development, public policies, international trade and South-South cooperation. He is an Agricultural Engineer, specialised in urban agriculture and phytopathology, with experience in the production of ornamental crops and the use of biological products to control plant disease and pests in vegetable production. His research interests include South-South cooperation, agricultural technical cooperation, paradiplomacy, national innovation systems and TICs and climate change. Email: horacio.rodvaz@gmail.com

Iván Roberto Sierra Medel has published extensively on international development cooperation topics since 1996. A career member of the Mexican Foreign Service, he was appointed Ambassador to the Cooperative Republic of Guyana in 2015. Previously, he was senior foreign policy advisor to the office of the President of Mexico and advisor to the Minister of Foreign Affairs. His previous diplomatic posts include Panama, Malaysia, and the Consulate General of Mexico in Sacramento, California. He has been a lecturer at Mexico's Autonomous Institute of Technology ITAM, Instituto Mora, Universidad de las Americas, and Universidad de Guadalajara. He earned an M.A. in Diplomacy at Mexico's Matias Romero Institute and both a B.A. and an M.A. in Philology at Moscow State University, Russia. Email: isierra68@yahoo.com